The Bahamas

A TASTE OF THE ISLANDS

Paris Permenter & John Bigley

HUNTER

HUNTER PUBLISHING, INC.
130 Campus Drive, Edison, NJ 08818
☎ 732-225-1900; 800-255-0343; fax 732-417-1744
hunterp@bellsouth.net
www.hunterpublishing.com

Ulysses Travel Publications
4176 Saint-Denis, Montréal, Québec
Canada H2W 2M5
☎ 514-843-9882 ext 2232; fax 514-843-9448

Windsor Books
The Boundary, Wheatley Road, Garsington
Oxford, OX44 9EJ England
☎ 01865-361122; fax 01865-361133

ISBN 1-55650-832-8
© 2000 Paris Permenter & John Bigley

Cover image: Beach bar at Atlantis Paradise Island
© Paris Permenter & John Bigley
All other images © Paris Permenter & John Bigley
unless otherwise specified
Maps by Kim André © 2000 Hunter Publishing, Inc.

1   2   3   4

www.hunterpublishing.com

Hunter's full range of guides to all corners of the globe is featured on our exciting website. You'll find guidebooks to suit every type of traveler, no matter what their budget, lifestyle, or idea of fun. Log on and join the excitement!

Adventure Guides – There are now over 40 titles in this series, covering destinations from Costa Rica and the Yucatán to Florida's West Coast, New Hampshire and the Alaska Highway. Complete information on what to do, as well as where to stay and eat, *Adventure Guides* are tailor-made for the active traveler, with a focus on hiking, biking, canoeing, horseback riding, trekking, skiing, watersports and all other kinds of fun.

Alive Guides – This ever-popular line of books takes a unique look at the best each destination offers: fine dining, nightlife, first-class hotels and resorts. In-margin icons direct the reader at a glance. Top-sellers include: *The Cayman Islands, St. Martin & St. Barts,* and *Aruba, Bonaire & Curaçao.*

Our *Romantic Weekends* guidebooks provide a series of escapes for couples of all ages and lifestyles. Unlike most "romantic" travel books, ours cover more than charming hotels and delightful restaurants, featuring a host of activities that you and your partner will remember forever.

Non-series travel books available from Hunter include *Best Dives of the Western Hemisphere; Golf Resorts; The Jewish Travel Guide; Chile & Easter Island Travel Companion* and many more.

Full descriptions are given for each book, along with reviewers' comments and a cover image. Books may be purchased on-line using our secure transaction facility.

About the Authors

John and Paris are professional travel writers and photographers specializing in the Caribbean. The team contribute travel articles and photographs to many top magazines and newspapers.

In addition to their nine titles written for Hunter, they are the authors of *Gourmet Getaways: A Taste of North America's Top Resorts*, *Texas Getaways for Two*, *Day Trips from San Antonio and Austin*, and *Texas Barbecue*, named Best Regional Guidebook by the Mid-America Publishers Association. The couple are frequent radio and TV talk show guests and have appeared on several travel shows.

Both Paris and John are members of the prestigious Society of American Travel Writers (SATW) and the American Society of Journalists and Authors (ASJA). The husband-wife team reside in Texas Hill Country, near Austin. More about the couple's travels can be found at www.parisandjohn.com.

Contents

☷ ᴍaps

Area Code

The area code for the Bahamas is 242.

Hurricane Floyd

In September of 1999, the Islands of the Bahamas were hit by Hurricane Floyd. The islands that sustained the heaviest damage were Abaco, Cat Island and Eleuthera; some damage was also reported on San Salvador, Exuma, New Providence and Grand Bahama.

At press time, damage estimates were still coming in, although the response has been speedy. Transportation, communications and a business-as-usual attitude have returned already on most islands.

So, should you reconsider your trip here? Not at all. Reconstruction is underway as we write; hopefully, by the time you read this all facilities will be up and running even better than before. We do suggest that you make some preliminary calls before you head to the islands. Call the tourism offices as well as accommodations to learn about their status. We've tried to obtain updates on properties, restaurants and attractions but changes are being made on a daily basis.

A huge response for disaster relief also helped the regeneration. If you would like to learn more about donating to relief efforts, contact: The National Headquarters of the Bahamas Red Cross Society, No. 24 John F. Kennedy Drive, PO Box N-8331, Nassau, The Bahamas. ☎ 242/323-7370; fax 242/323-7404; e-mail info@Bahamas RedCross.org.

The Bahamas

Introduction

The islands of The Bahamas are scattered like tossed seashells in the relatively shallow waters just east of Florida's shore. In all, there are over 700 islands and over 2,000 small cays and islets that make up The Bahamas, spread out across 100,000 square miles. Only 20 of these landforms are populated.

The Bahamas enjoy a Caribbean climate due to the nearby Gulf Stream, a current of warm water that was discovered by Ponce de Leon while searching for the Fountain of Youth. The Gulf Stream certainly bestows a youthful feeling on those lucky enough to take a dip in its waters. But these islands are technically not part of the Caribbean, so expect slightly cooler water temperatures during the winter months.

"Bahamas"

The name Bahamas comes from "bajar mar" or "shallow sea," a name given to the island chain by the Spanish over 500 years ago.

History

The first residents of these islands were the Lucayan Indians. Historians believed these settlers traveled to the region from South America around the ninth century AD and lived a quiet, peaceful existence until European discovery in 1492. Historians still debate exactly where Columbus first made landfall, but one long-held theory is that his introduction to the New World was at the Bahamian island of San Salvador.

The Spanish held the islands until 1718 when the British laid claim to this area following a quarter-century of upheaval. For years the islands served as a hideout for pirates; later they became known as a place from which to smuggle Confederate goods in and out of the South during the Civil War.

The Union Jack flew over these islands until The Bahamas became an independent nation. Today, the Islands of The Bahamas is an independent member of the Commonwealth of Nations; the Queen is the constitutional head of state.

Planning Your Trip

Keep in mind that the Islands of The Bahamas is not one destination, but hundreds. Scattered across a vast region, these many islands offer a diverse assortment of destinations.

So where should you go? The decision will depend on many factors:

- ☀ How long can you stay? If this is a quick getaway of just three or four nights, select a destination that's easy to reach, like Nassau or Freeport.

- ☀ How much seclusion do you want? If it's peace and quiet you're after, move past the main tourist spots such as Nassau and Freeport in favor of quieter get-aways, such as Bimini, Eleuthera and others.

☀ What type of accommodations do you want? Are you looking for an all-inclusive, a small inn, or something in-between? Most all-inclusives are found in Nassau. Small inns are found on almost all of the inhabited islands.

⁘ Accommodation Types

Whatever you're looking for in the way of accommodations – high-rise hotel, seaside bungalow, bed and breakfast, small traditional hotel, or private villa – you'll find it in The Bahamas.

Just as varied as the type of accommodations is the range of prices of these properties. Everything from budget motels with spartan furnishings to private islands that attract royalty and Hollywood types is available.

This guidebook covers things in-between, places where the everyday vacationers can enjoy safety and comfort. The resorts, hotels and villas featured on these pages offer all levels of activity. Some strive to offer around-the-clock fun and evening theme parties for their guests; others point the way for guests to find their own entertainment. Some are located on the beach; others up the mountains with grandiose views. Some are full-service properties with everything from beauty salons to jewelry shops to a half-dozen bars and restaurants located right on the property; others are simple accommodations where the guests enjoy dinner in former greathouses built over 200 years ago.

Choosing a Bahamian accommodation that is right for you is important. You'll find that an island resort, unlike a property in a downtown US city, for example, becomes your home away from home. This is not just where you spend your nights, but also a good portion of your days, languishing on the beach, lying beneath towering palms and luxuriating in a warm sea.

What form will your paradise take? A resort with daily activities and a pulsating nightlife? A historic inn furnished with Caribbean antiques? Or a quiet getaway where the only footprints are your own?

The choice is yours.

Abaco Beach Resort & Boat Harbor.

All-Inclusive Resorts

As the name suggests, all-inclusive means that all activities, meals, drinks, transfers and tips are included in the price.

This policy gives you the opportunity try anything you like without worrying about blowing your vacation budget for the next five years. Ever been curious about windsurfing? Take a lesson. Want to know how to reggae dance? Throw off your shoes and jump in line. Wonder how those brightly colored drinks with the funny umbrellas taste? Belly up to the bar. You're free to try it all.

Some folks don't like all-inclusive because of the concern (not unfounded) that once you've paid for the whole package you'll be unlikely to leave the property to sample local restaurants and explore the island.

We love all-inclusive resorts, but we are careful to balance a stay there with island tours or visits to off-property restaurants. Even with these extra expenditures, we've found most of these resorts to be economical choices. Top all-inclusive choices in The Bahamas include several Club Med facilities, Breezes Bahamas (part of Jamaica's SuperClubs chain), Sandals Royal Bahamian Resort and Spa (a member of Jamaica's popular Sandals chain) and many properties with meals-only plans (i.e., not drinks or watersports). In the Turks and Caicos, all-inclusive resorts include Club Med and Beaches.

Intimate Inns

If you're looking for peace and quiet, small inns offer good getaways and a chance to immerse yourself in more of the local atmosphere. It's that opportunity to meet local residents, taste island dishes and retreat from the typical resort experience that brings travelers to The Bahamas' often overlooked small inns.

Island Outpost

Several small inns in The Bahamas are part of Island Outpost, a collection of small properties throughout the Caribbean headed up by Chris Blackwell. "I am really keen on the development and promotion of small inns," said Chris Blackwell, owner and founder of the Island Records label that brought Bob Marley to fame. In The Bahamas, Island Outpost properties include Pink Sands and Compass Point.

Just as you would if booking a B&B in the US, ask plenty of questions before making reservations in a small inn. These properties may offer limited services and may be more restrictive. If applicable, be sure to ask:

- Is smoking permitted indoors?
- Are children allowed as guests?
- Is breakfast served at one time or as guests wander in?
- Are intimate tables available or are meals served family style?
- Are special dietary considerations met?
- Is there a minimum stay?
- Does a remote location necessitate a rental car?

Villas

For some travelers, the idea of real getaway is to immerse themselves in the island, to feel as if they are residents. One of the best ways to do this, especially if you're enjoying an extended stay, is to rent a villa.

Villas vary in price, services and level of luxury. Before you make a commitment, check:

- Maid service. Many villas offer maid service before your arrival and after your departure; additional cleaning can be arranged for a surcharge. At other properties, you may have daily maid service included. Check with your villa management company.
- Groceries. Can you send a deposit for groceries and have a cook stock up before your arrival? Finding a refrigerator and cabinets filled with your favorites can be a big boost after a long flight.
- Cook service. Many villas can arrange for cook service as you choose: three meals a day, dinner only, or just one special meal. Check your options.
- Air conditioning. Don't assume your villa is air-conditioned; ever-present trade winds make this an optional feature. If it's more of a necessity than an option to you, be sure to ask about it.
- Car rental. Many villas are located away from the resort areas. See if you should rent a car to avoid pricey taxi rides for long hauls.

☀ Minimum stay. Unlike hotel minimums of three nights, villas often require a minimum seven-night rental.

Travelers' Information

Banking

On the larger islands (New Providence Island in Nassau and Paradise Island and Freeport/Lucaya on Grand Bahama Island) the banks are open from 9:30 am to 3 pm, Monday through Thursday, and 9:30 to 5 on Friday. Hours are more abbreviated on the Out Islands (those islands beyond New Providence and Grand Bahama).

Climate

The Bahamas does not always share in the Caribbean climate enjoyed by its southern neighbors. While the Gulf Stream does keep these islands temperate, remember that technically they are not part of the Caribbean and can feel the chill of a winter from time to time. The average high temperature is 80°. Winter temperatures hover in the 70s, dropping to about 60° at night. Summer months find a rise in mercury with temperatures approaching the high 80s. The rainy season is May through October. Hurricane season extends from June through November.

Spring Break

In deciding when to visit The Bahamas, people carefully consider the weather. Be sure to factor in another important item, however: spring break. Thousands of students descend upon the islands (especially to the cities of Nassau and Freeport) from late February through early April. If you want a quiet getaway, keep this in mind.

Crime

As in any big city, crime is a problem in Nassau and, to a lesser degree, in Freeport. Away from these areas, the crime rate is lower, but vacationers should still take commonsense precautions. Do not leave valuables on the beach while you go for a swim, no matter how secluded the beach.

Currency

The Bahamian dollar is the legal tender of the islands. It is set at an exchange rate to be on par with the US dollar. Visitors from the States don't need to worry about changing money, however; the US dollar is legal tender throughout the islands.

Credit Cards

Major credit cards are accepted at most establishments.

Customs Regulations

Travelers arriving in The Bahamas may bring 50 cigars, 200 cigarettes or one pound of tobacco, one quart of spirits and personal effects. Only canned fruit or canned or frozen meats can be imported. US Customs will allow travelers to bring back US $600 worth of merchandise duty free. A 10% tax is charged on the next $1,000 worth of goods. US citizens may mail home gifts of up to $50 without duty and may also take back one liter of wine or liquor and five cartons of cigarettes duty free.

Departure Tax

A departure tax of $15 per person is charged from Nassau/Paradise Island and the Out Islands. The departure tax from Grand Bahama Island is $18 per person. Children under six years are exempted from payment of departure tax with proof of age.

Dress

With its strong British history, the citizens of The Bahamas are modest, conservative people who generally frown upon displays of skin. Most islanders follow a more conservative style of dress than seen in US beach communities.

Bathing suits are appropriate only for swimming; when off the beach grab a cover-up. Bare chests (for both women and men) are also frowned upon off the beach. However, leisure wear – T-shirts, shorts, sundresses and sandals –will be readily accepted in any Caribbean community.

Throughout this book, we've included dress code suggestions for all restaurants. Expect high season (mid-December through mid-April) to be the dressiest period, the only time when jackets and occasionally ties will be required at a few restaurants for dinner. Generally, "casually elegant" or "resort casual" is the order of the day, an indication that it's fine to wear polo shirts, khakis and sundresses.

Driving

A valid US driver's license or an international driver's may be used. (US licenses may be used for up to three months only.) All driving is on the left.

Drugs

Marijuana is illegal throughout The Bahamas. Drug penalties are becoming stiffer and drug prevention measures more stringent. We also caution vacationers not to return home with any packages that they have not personally packed. We were once approached in the Turks and Caicos airport by a driver who asked us to mail a package for him when we reached Miami. The request may have been legitimate, but the risk is too great.

Electricity

Throughout the islands, electricity is 120 volts AC.

Embassies

While in The Bahamas, an American Embassy can be found at Queen Street in Nassau; ☎ 242/322-1181 or 242/328-2206.

If you would like to contact the Bahamian embassy in the US, the address is: Embassy of The Bahamas, 2220 Massachusetts Avenue, N.W., Washington, DC 20008. ☎ 202/319-2660.

Entry Requirements

US citizens must carry proof of citizenship (passport or certified birth certificate and photo identification). Voter registration cards are not accepted as proof of citizenship. Visas are not required for stays shorter than eight months.

You will be issued an immigration card when entering The Bahamas. Hold onto it; you will need to present the card upon departure. When departing, you'll clear US Customs and Immigration in Nassau or Freeport, a real time-saver.

Immunizations

No immunizations are required to travel to the Islands of The Bahamas.

Information Sources

Web site. For more information on the Islands of The Bahamas, check out www.bahamas.com. For specifics on the Out Islands, try www.bahama-out-islands.com.

Language

English, spoken with a Bahamian lilt, is used throughout the islands.

Marriage

There's no better excuse for a feast than a wedding, and getting married in the Islands of The Bahamas is a simple task. The regulations are:

☀ One of the parties must physically be in the country at the time the marriage application is made.

☀ One of the parties must reside in the Islands of The Bahamas for one day prior to the marriage.

☀ If either party is divorced, the original final decree or a finalized copy of the divorce must be presented to the Clerk of the Court.

☀ If either party is widowed, the original or notarized copy of the death certificate must be presented.

☀ Parties under age 18 must have parental consent; US citizens under 18 must produce a declaration certifying this fact before the US Consul at the American Embassy in Nassau.

No blood test is necessary; the marriage license fee is $40. Most larger hotels have wedding consultants on staff to help take care of paperwork or you can file directly with the office of the Registrar General in Nassau (weekdays 9:30 to 4:30). When the license is granted, the commissioner's office on the island where the marriage will take place is notified of the upcoming event. If you have questions, contact the Tourism Office or ☎ 888/NUPTIAL.

Pets

Pet owners need to obtain an approved permit from the Ministry of Agriculture and Fisheries to bring any animal into the country. You can write to the Director of Agriculture, Attention: Permit Section, PO Box N-3704, Nassau, Bahamas. Include a letter with your full name and address and expected arrival date, final destination in the Islands of The Bahamas and information on the pet (species, breed, age, sex, etc.). All pets must be six months or older. The application fee is $10.

Photography

Ask permission before taking photos. In some of the market areas (especially Nassau's Straw Market) you will be expected to make a purchase before taking a photo.

Public Holidays

National holidays are New Year's Day, Good Friday, Easter, Whit Monday (the last Monday in May), Labour Day (first Monday in June), Independence Day (July 10), Emancipation Day (first Monday in August), Discovery Day (Oct. 12), Christmas Day and Boxing Day (Dec. 26).

Telephones

Good telephone service is available from The Bahamas. The area code is 242.

You can bring along your cell phone to use in the islands, but you'll need to register it with The Bahamas Telecommunications Corporation, ☎ 242/394-4000 or fax 242/394-3573.

Time Zone

All the Islands of The Bahamas are on Eastern Standard Time. From April through October the islands change to Eastern Daylight Time.

Tipping

You'll find that the service charge is often (make that usually) added to the bill at most restaurants. If not, a 10-15% tip is customary. Remember that tips are part of the package at many all-inclusive resorts; check with yours. Tips are generally not expected for short taxi rides.

Tourism Offices

For information on The Bahamas, call toll-free ☎ 800/8-BAHAMAS within the United States. From Canada, the toll-free number is ☎ 800/677-3777. For additional information, contact the office nearest you.

In the US

Chicago office: 8600 Bryn Mawr Avenue, Suite 820, Chicago, IL 60631, ☎ 773/693-1500.

Dallas office: World Trade Center, Suite 116, 2050 Stemmons Freeway, P.O. Box 581408, Dallas, TX 75258-1408, ☎ 214/742-1886.

Los Angeles office: 3450 Wilshire Boulevard, Suite 208, Los Angeles, CA 90010, ☎ 213/385-0033.

Miami office: One Turnberry Place, 19495 Biscayne Boulevard, Suite 242, Aventura, FL 33180, ☎ 305/932-0051.

New York office: 150 East 52nd Street, 28th Floor North, New York, NY 10022, ☎ 212/758-2777.

Toronto office: 121 Bloor Street East, Suite 1101, Toronto, Ontario M4W 3M5, ☎ 416/968-2999.

Specific Island Offices

Bahamas Out Islands Promotion Board, 1100 Lee Wagener Blvd., Suite 204, Fort Lauderdale, FL 33315; ☎ 800/688-4752.

Grand Bahama Island Tourism Board, One Turnberry Place, 19495 Biscayne Blvd., Suite 809, Aventura, FL 33180; ☎ 800/448-3386.

Nassau/Paradise Island Promotion Board, One Turnberry Place, 19495 Biscayne Blvd, Suite 804, Aventura, FL 33180; ☎ 800/327-9019.

Water

Water is safe to drink, although bottled water will be served on many of the Out Islands.

Weather

Check out The Bahamas Department of Meteorology's Website at http://flamingo.bahamas.net.bs/weather.

Getting There

☀ Arriving By Air

Abaco

American Eagle, ☎ 800/433-7300. Flights from Miami to Marsh Harbour.

BahamasAir, ☎ 800/222-4262. Flights from West Palm Beach to Marsh Harbour; domestic flights from Nassau and Grand Bahama Island.

Continental Connection, ☎ 800/231-0856. Flights from Ft. Lauderdale and Miami to Marsh Harbour; flights from Ft. Lauderdale and Miami to Treasure Cay.

Island Express, ☎ 954/359-0380. Flights from Ft. Lauderdale to Marsh Harbour and Treasure Cay.

Twin Air, ☎ 954/359-8266. Flights from Ft Lauderdale to Treasure Cay.

USAirways Express, ☎ 800/428-4322. Flights from West Palm Beach to Marsh Harbour and Treasure Cay; flights from Orlando to Treasure Cay.

Walker's International, ☎ 800/925-5377. Flights from Ft. Lauderdale to Walker's Cay.

Acklins

BahamasAir, ☎ 800/222-4262. Domestic flights from Nassau.

Andros

BahamasAir, ☎ 800/222-4262. Domestic flights from Nassau and Grand Bahama Island.

Bimini

BahamasAir, ☎ 800/222-4262. Domestic flights from Nassau and Grand Bahama Island.

Bimini Island Air, ☎ 954/938-9524. Flights from Miami to South Bimini; flights from Ft. Lauderdale to South Bimini. No scheduled service, charter only.

Island Air Charters, ☎ 305/359-9942. Flights from Ft. Lauderdale to South Bimini. No scheduled service, charter only.

Cat Island

BahamasAir, ☎ 800/222-4262. Domestic flights from Nassau.

Crooked Island

BahamasAir, ☎ 800/222-4262. Domestic flights from Nassau.

Eleuthera

American Eagle, ☎ 800/433-7300. Service from Miami to Governor's Harbour.

BahamasAir, ☎ 800/222-4262. Service from Miami to Governor's Harbour; domestic flights from Nassau and Grand Bahama Island.

Continental Connection, ☎ 800/231-0861. Service from Miami and Ft. Lauderdale to North Eleuthera.

USAirways Express, ☎ 800/428-4322. Service from Ft. Lauderdale to Governor's Harbour.

Exuma

American Eagle, ☎ 800/433-7300. Service from Miami to Exuma.

BahamasAir, ☎ 800/222-4262. Service from Miami to Exuma.

Grand Bahama Island

American Eagle, ☎ 800/433-7300. Service from Miami to Freeport.

BahamasAir, ☎ 800/222-4262. Service from Miami to Freeport.

Continental Connection, ☎ 800/231-0856. Service from Miami, Ft. Lauderdale and West Palm Beach to Freeport.

Inagua, Long Island & Mayaguana

BahamasAir, ☎ 800/222-4262. Domestic flights from Nassau.

New Providence Island (Nassau/Paradise Island)

Air Canada, ☎ 800/776-3000. Service from Toronto and Montreal to Nassau.

Air Jamaica, ☎ 800/523-5585. Service from Montego Bay to Nassau.

American Eagle, ☎ 800/433-7300. Service from Miami and Orlando to Nassau.

BahamasAir, ☎ 800/222-4262. Service from Miami, Ft. Lauderdale and Orlando to Nassau.

British Airways, ☎ 800/247-9297. Service from London to Nassau.

Comair, ☎ 800/241-1212. Service from Orlando to Nassau.

Continental Connection, ☎ 800/231-0856. Service from Miami, Ft. Lauderdale and West Palm Beach to Nassau.

Delta Air Lines, ☎ 800/241-4141. Service from Atlanta, New York, DFW to Nassau.

Paradise Islands Airways, ☎ 800/SUN-7202. Service from Miami, Ft. Lauderdale and West Palm Beach to Nassau.

USAirways, ☎ 800/428-4322. Service from Charlotte and Philadelphia to Nassau.

San Salvador

BahamasAir, ☎ 800/222-4262. Service from Miami to San Salvador.

❖ Arriving By Cruise Ship

The cruise industry brings thousands of vacationers to The Bahamas every year. Many travel from Port Canaveral or Miami and stop in Nassau or Freeport for a day of shopping and beach fun; others such as the Royal Caribbean Cruise Line make stops at the smaller Berry islands and CoCo Cay. Princess Cruises makes a stop in Eleuthera. A lot of these cruises are seasonal; check with the cruise lines for their most recent scheduled stops.

Carnival Cruise Lines - - - - - - - - - - ☎ 800/327-9501
Celebrity Cruises - - - - - - - - - - - - - - ☎ 800/437-3111
Costa Cruise Lines - - - - - - - - - - - - - ☎ 800/462-6782
Crystal Cruises - - - - - - - - - - - - - - ☎ 800/-5-CUNARD
Disney Cruise Line - - - - - - - - - - - - - ☎ 800/951-3532
Dolphin Cruise Line - - - - - - - - - - - - ☎ 800/222-1003
Holland America Cruise Line - - - - - - ☎ 206/281-0351
Majesty Cruise Line - - - - - - - - - - - - ☎ 800/532-7788
Norwegian - - - - - - - - - - - - - - - - - - ☎ 800/327-7030
Premier Cruise Lines - - - - - - - - - - - ☎ 800/327-7113
Princess Cruises - - - - - - - - - - - - - - ☎ 800/421-0522
Regal Cruises - - - - - - - - - - - - - - - - ☎ 800/270-7245
Royal Caribbean Cruise Line - - - - - - ☎ 800/327-6700
Royal Olympic Cruises - - - - - - - - - - ☎ 800/872-6400
Seabourn Cruise Line - - - - - - - - - - - ☎ 800/929-9595
Silversea Cruises - - - - - - - - - - - - - - ☎ 800/722-6655

The Bahamas

Getting Around

⁙ Travel By Taxi

With driving on the left, which may be uncomfortable for US visitors, taxi and limo service are the top way to get around these islands. Rates are set at $2.20 for the first quarter-mile for one or two passengers. Every additional quarter-mile will be charged at 30 cents per mile. Additional passengers pay $3 per person (kids under three travel free).

Cab Fares

On New Providence Island, expect to pay about $15 to get from the airport to Cable Beach, $20 for a ride downtown, or $24 (plus a $2 bridge toll) to reach Paradise Island.

⁙ Travel By Bus

Public minibuses called jitneys are an inexpensive mode of transportation and a great way to experience local life. (Although not the best choice if you're in a hurry.) On New Providence Island, jitneys run from downtown near the Hilton British Colonial and from Cable Beach. Jitneys also serve Freeport. Rides start at 75¢ (have correct money because drivers don't give change).

⁙ Rental Cars

Remember that you must drive on the left. This can be tricky for newcomers and a real challenge in heavily trafficked areas such as Nassau.

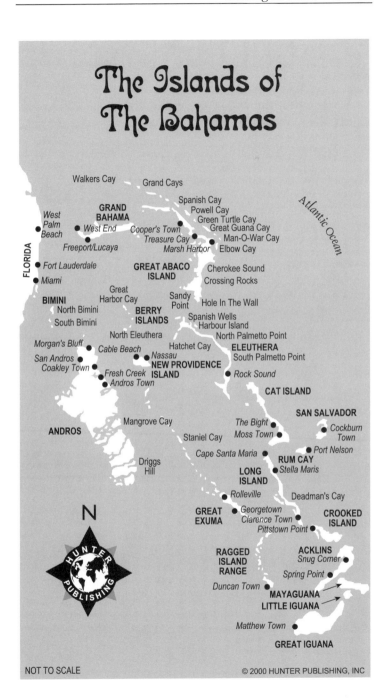

The Islands of The Bahamas

Walkers Cay   Grand Cays

Spanish Cay
Powell Cay
Green Turtle Cay
Great Guana Cay
Man-O-War Cay
Elbow Cay

West Palm Beach

GRAND BAHAMA
West End   Cooper's Town
Treasure Cay
Marsh Harbor

Freeport/Lucaya

FLORIDA

Fort Lauderdale
Miami

GREAT ABACO ISLAND

Cherokee Sound
Crossing Rocks

BIMINI
North Bimini
South Bimini

Great Harbor Cay

BERRY ISLANDS

Sandy Point   Hole In The Wall

Spanish Wells
Harbour Island

North Eleuthera

North Palmetto Point

Morgan's Bluff   Cable Beach   Hatchet Cay

San Andros
Coakley Town

Nassau
NEW PROVIDENCE ISLAND

Fresh Creek
Andros Town

ELEUTHERA
South Palmetto Point

Rock Sound

CAT ISLAND

SAN SALVADOR

ANDROS

Mangrove Cay

Staniel Cay

The Bight
Moss Town

Cockburn Town

Port Nelson

Cape Santa Maria

Driggs Hill

RUM CAY
Stella Maris

LONG ISLAND

Rolleville

Deadman's Cay

N

GREAT EXUMA

Georgetown
Clarence Town
Pittstown Point

CROOKED ISLAND

HUNTER PUBLISHING

RAGGED ISLAND RANGE

Duncan Town

ACKLINS
Snug Corner

Spring Point

MAYAGUANA
LITTLE IGUANA

Matthew Town

GREAT IGUANA

Atlantic Ocean

NOT TO SCALE

© 2000 HUNTER PUBLISHING, INC

The Bahamas

If you want to rent a car, you must be 17 years of age and possess a valid driver's license. (US licenses may be used for up to three months.)

Cost of a rental car varies, but expect to pay somewhere between $45 and $85 per day, depending on model. Major rental car companies can be found in Nassau and Freeport in both the airports and major hotels. Costs are higher on the Out Islands (and don't expect that a tank of gas will be included with your rental on these smaller islands).

☼ Other Options

Motor scooters are also available for rent on some of the islands for those brave enough to head out on two wheels. Helmets are mandatory. Expect to pay as much as $50 per day (you may also rent for a half-day).

Bicycles can be found on some islands as well. Ask around.

Shopping

Shopping in The Bahamas is part of the total experience, especially if you move away from the stores aimed at tourists to enter the world of Bahamian commerce. Leave the resort gift shops (where markup is fierce) and head to local grocery stores and markets for a true taste of Bahamian life.

Bargaining is part of the fun at the many craft markets throughout the island. A lot of travelers avoid the market, fearing high-pressure sales, but we have found the atmosphere to be delightful. A friendly "good morning," abstaining from photos until a purchase (no matter how small) is made and general good manners will go far with the salespeople.

The largest selection of shops is found in **Nassau** and **Freeport**. Shops in Nassau are generally open 9 am-5 pm,

Monday to Saturdays. In Grand Bahama, shops at Lucaya Marketplace and the International Bazaar are open 10 am-6 pm, Monday to Saturday.

The Bahamas

Tastes of
The Bahamas

On a visit to The Bahamas, especially its larger islands of New Providence and Grand Bahama, you may wonder just what Bahamian cuisine is. With a deluge of international restaurants as well as fast food establishments, it sometimes seems that The Bahamas offers a taste of any type of food you want, which it does.

But these islands also boast their own unique cuisine, dishes that feature fresh local seafood and plenty of spices.

One of the main ingredients found on a Bahamian menu is **conch** (pronounced konk). You're probably familiar with this mollusk because of its shell: a beautiful pink curl nearly a foot long that, when blown by those in the know, can become an island bullhorn. The conch are caught in the sea (and, in the Turks and Caicos, farmed like catfish or crawfish on the mainland). The shell covers a huge piece of rubbery white meat, as well as a "foot," the appendage used by the conch to drag itself along the ocean floor in search of food. It is the white meat that makes up such a big chunk of the Bahamian menu. It is chopped, sliced, diced, fried, marinated and served just about every imaginable way.

To tenderize the conch, the chef scores the meat with a knife, soaks it with lime juice and spices and sometimes even pounds it. Conch recipes are numerous – cracked conch, conch salad, conch chowder, conch fritters. You name it, they serve it that way. (For more on these savory dishes, see *On the Menu*, pages 26 and 27.)

Another Bahamian favorite is the **rock lobster,** a clawless lobster that is served many ways. **Crabs** are also found on many menus, as are **grouper** and **snapper.**

If you are staying in a condo or accommodation with kitchen, you may want to purchase your own seafood and cook it up Bahamian-style. Do as the locals do and buy it right on the waterfront. In Nassau, seafood vendors can be found at:

☉ Potter's Cay, at the base of the Paradise Island Bridge

☉ Eastern Road on Montagu Beach

☉ Arawak Cay on West Bay Street

☉ Paradise Island dock

Prices are subject to good-natured haggling. Many stalls will prepare the conch Bahamian-style for you in a matter of minutes, dicing and spicing the raw conch with a marinade of peppers and onions (see *On the Menu*, page 27). Some vendors also sell cooked (often fried) seafood as well, including grouper, bonefish, snapper and crawfish or Bahamian lobster in season.

Real Taste of The Bahamas Program

If your goal is to search out real Bahamian cuisine, your task is now much easier thanks to the "Real Taste of The Bahamas" program. A cooperative effort of the Ministry of Tourism, the Ministry of Agriculture and Fisheries and the Restaurant Association of The Bahamas, this program seeks to promote independent restaurants that offer a quality dining experience while utilizing and showcasing indigenous food products. To join the program, restaurants must:

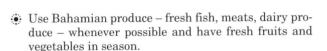

☀ Use Bahamian produce – fresh fish, meats, dairy produce – whenever possible and have fresh fruits and vegetables in season.

☀ Provide the highest standards of cleanliness in the dining rooms and kitchen.

☀ Have at least one staff member trained and knowledgeable about The Bahamas, a BahamaHost graduate.

☀ Treat guests with every possible courtesy.

☀ Provide the best possible service to patrons.

Identifying member restaurants is easy, thanks to the Real Taste of The Bahamas logo displayed by qualifying eateries. The banner, highlighted by a conch and pineapple, identifies members. For more on the program, contact the Real Taste of The Bahamas, PO Box N-3701, Nassau, New Providence, Bahamas or call ☎ 242/322-7500, Extension 2086. Here's a list of participating restaurants supplied by the Real Taste of The Bahamas:

Androsia, West Bay St., Cable Beach, ☎ 242/327-7805.

Anthony's Caribbean Grill, East Casino Drive, Paradise Island, ☎ 242/363-3152.

Avery's, Adelaide Village, ☎ 242/326-1547.

Bahamian Kitchen, Trinity Place, ☎ 242/325-0702.

Buena Vista, Deveaux Street off Bay St., ☎ 242/322-2811.

Café Johnny Canoe, West Bay Street, Cable Beach, ☎ 242/327-3373.

Capriccio, West Bay Street, ☎ 242/327-8547.

Comfort Zone, #5 Wulff Road, ☎ 242/323-2676.

Conch Fritters Bar and Grill, Marlborough Street, ☎ 242/323-8801.

Anthony's Caribbean Grill, East Casino Drive, Paradise Island, ☎ 242/363-3152.

Europe, West Bay Street, ☎ 242/322-8032.

Junkanoo Café, Colony Place Arcade, Bay Street, ☎ 242/328-7944.

Mama Lyddy's Place, Market St., ☎ 242/328-6849.
Montagu Gardens Steak and Grill, East Bay Street, ☎ 242/394-6347.
The Poop Deck, East Bay Street, ☎ 242/393-8175.
The Shoal, Nassau Street, ☎ 242/323-4400.
Stars Restaurant and Deli, Circle Palm Mall, Soldier Road, ☎ 242/394-1692.
Sun And..., Lakeview Rd. off Shirley St., ☎ 242/393-2644.
Tony Roma's, West Bay Street, ☎ 242/325-2020.
Travellers Rest, West Bay Street, ☎ 242/327-7633.

In The Market

Banana. The banana is a plant, not a tree, bearing only one bunch of bananas before it is cut down to allow a new shoot to take its place.

Club Med's Banana Fritters

- *1 cup all-purpose flour*
- *1½ teaspoon baking powder*
- *½ teaspoon salt*
- *4 eggs*
- *¼ pound mashed bananas*
- *2 teaspoons unsalted butter, melted and cooled*
- *2 teaspoons vegetable oil*
- *1 teaspoon rum*
- *1 tablespoon sugar*

Sift flour, baking powder, sugar and salt in bowl. Make a well in the center and add the eggs, butter, oil and rum. Beat thoroughly. Let batter stand for one or two hours before using. Add bananas. Heat additional vegetable oil in a deep fryer to 370°. Drop fritter mixture by tablespoonful into hot fat and cook until golden brown. Drain on paper towels. *Makes about 24 fritters.* ☀

Calabeza. This is the West Indian pumpkin, a small, nonsweet vegetable that is used like an acorn squash in soups and stews. If you can't find calabeza at home, substitute acorn, Hubbard, or butternut squash.

Callaloo. This leafy vegetable resembles spinach and is used similarly. Don't miss the callaloo soup, usually spiced up with saltfish. The vegetable originally comes from India but is seen often in the Caribbean these days. Substitutes for callaloo include spinach, Swiss chard and Chinese pak choy.

Carambola. The carambola is often called starfruit, a reference to its distinctive shape. A waxy fruit that can be eaten raw, either sliced or in a fruit salad, the shape of the light green fruit is easily seen when cut in cross section.

Chicken foot. Just as it sounds, this is the foot of a chicken. It is used to flavor soups and stews, especially in hard times.

Cho-Cho. This member of the squash family is known as chayote or christophene on some islands. It can be served boiled or used in dishes. Don't have any cho-cho? Substitute a squash in the recipe instead.

Coconut. The coconut is a ubiquitous part of the Bahamian diet, used for everything from its milk to its meat to its brown shell.

Coconut Milk. Not to be confused with coconut water (which is the clear liquid that pours out of a cracked coconut), this milk is "harvested" by squeezing grated coconut that has been soaked in water. The sweet juice is used in baking and mixing drinks. Herbalists say the milk purifies the heart and washes the kidneys.

Coconut Milk

- *1 coconut*

Break coconut with a hammer and remove white meat with a knife. Grate the meat and add it to one pint of hot water. To extract the coconut milk, press through a sieve. Discard meat and refrigerate milk until used. ☀

The Bahamas

Dasheen. This root vegetable, called taro in the Pacific, is used much like a potato in soups. Sometimes it is called a coco yam.

Grouper. This large fish makes its appearance on just about every restaurant menu. The mild fish is served broiled, fried and just about every other imaginable way. (For grouper recipes, see pages 52, 54, 87, 122 and 190.)

Guava. These small fruits are used in desserts such as ice cream, fruit sauces and jellies. Usually the fruit has been blended because of the many pesky seeds.

Guineps. These small green fruits look somewhat like a small lime. To eat one, pop the flesh out from the skin and suck on it (don't eat the seed).

Hog Plum. These small plums are yellow or orange and are in season in the fall months. They taste a little like mango.

Jelly Coconut. The jelly coconut is an immature coconut that yields a clear, sweet jelly. Streetside vendors will whack the coconut with a machete, carving a chunk for you to use as an impromptu spoon to scoop out the cold jelly. Look for directional signs for jelly coconut as you drive the countryside for a taste of sweet goodness.

The Caribbean lobster has no claws.

Lobster. Nope, we're not talking Maine lobsters here, but the Bahamian rock lobster or crawfish that make an appearance on many menus. The obvious difference between the two? This southern cousin from warmer climes has no claws.

Lobster Linguine, Atlantic Beach Hotel

- *6 uncooked lobster tails*
- *2 pounds linguine*
- *1 medium onion, sliced*
- *3 garlic cloves*
- *2 tablespoons chopped basil*
- *16 ounces tomato sauce*
- *¼ cup white wine or brandy*
- *¼ cup heavy cream*
- *¼ cup chicken bouillon*
- *¼ cup olive oil*
- *salt and crushed red pepper to taste*
- *grated Parmesan cheese*

Cook and drain linguine. Sauté onion and garlic in oil with basil and crushed pepper. Boil lobster tails for 12-15 minutes, until white and firm. Remove meat from shell, dice and add to sautéed herbs. Add tomato sauce and wine or brandy, simmering for five minutes. Add bouillon and cook for three minutes. Add cream and cook for 30 seconds. Sprinkle with grated Parmesan cheese. *Serves 4 to 6.* ❀

■ ■

Mamey Sapote. This football-shaped fruit is in season all summer. Its pink flesh can be used for making preserves or eaten raw. Mango, peach or soursop are often substituted.

Mango. Long with flat sides, the mango is used in many desserts or, in its green stage, in chutneys and stews. Can't find mangoes in your local store? Substitute a peach.

Club Med Mango Appetizer

- *1 cup cold water*
- *2 cloves garlic, crushed*
- *½ teaspoon salt*
- *fresh ground pepper*
- *1 or more fresh hot green peppers, chopped*
- *¼ cup lime juice*

Mix all ingredients in blender. Dip sliced mangos into sauce as appetizer. ❀

■ ■ ■ ■ ■ ■ ■ ■ ■ ■ ■ ■ ■ ■ ■ ■ ■ ■ ■

The Bahamas

Oxtail. The oxtail, the tail of a cow, is used to flavor many soups and stews.

Passionfruit. This lovely fruit is used for drinks and ice cream.

Plantains. Don't get plantains mixed up with bananas. They may look similar, but the plantain is not an overgrown banana and tastes nothing like its sweet cousin. Plantains are used in recipes as a potato would be. They are often served sliced and fried. (For a plantain soup recipe, see page 58.)

Pumpkin. Unlike our sweet pumpkin, this West Indian pumpkin is a small, nonsweet vegetable that is used like an acorn squash. If you can't find a West Indian pumpkin (or calabeza) at home, substitute acorn, Hubbard, or butternut squash.

Sapodilla. Often called a dilly, the sapodilla is a fruit with sweet segments, and is eaten like an orange. Their season extends from March to early summer.

Snapper. Red and yellowtail snapper are favorite offerings and are caught by local fishermen.

Soursop. This green fruit is used to make drinks, ice cream and other desserts.

Sugar apple. Ripening in late summer and continuing until winter, the sugar apple requires some work to eat. The outer segments are pulled off and eaten to reveal sweet white flesh. Toss away the skin and seeds.

Spices of The Bahamas

The spices grown on this island give its cuisine the distinctive flavors that make Bahamian meals a special event.

Annatto. This spice, a derivative of a shrub, is used like saffron in soups, stews and other dishes. It gives food a red color.

Curry. This combination of many spices (turmeric, cardamom, cumin, cinnamon, mace and others) flavors many dishes in The Bahamas.

Escallion. This member of the onion family frequently appears in many Bahamian recipes. If you can't find escallion, substitute green onion tops.

Nutmeg. Order a rum punch in most island bars and you'll have a look at a popular use of nutmeg: sprinkled on top of the potent drink. Nutmeg is a popular spice on these islands. The tree grows naturally throughout the island and produces a seed, called the nutmeg. A red, stringy covering around the seed is called mace.

Vanilla. The vanilla bean comes from the vanilla plant, an orchid.

Substitution Chart

If you can't find some of the Caribbean ingredients in your local supermarket, try substituting these items in recipes:

Pumpkin/calabeza acorn ~ Hubbard/butternut squash

Callaloo ~ ~ ~ ~ ~ ~ ~ ~ ~ ~ ~ spinach or pak choy

Cho-cho squash ~ ~ ~ christophene or chayote squash

Dasheen ~ ~ ~ ~ ~ ~ ~ ~ ~ ~ ~ ~ ~ ~ ~ potato

Mango ~ ~ ~ ~ ~ ~ ~ ~ ~ ~ ~ ~ ~ ~ ~ ~ peach

Scotch bonnet ~ ~ ~ ~ ~ ~ ~ hot pepper of your choice

Escallion ~ ~ ~ ~ ~ ~ ~ ~ ~ ~ ~ green onion tips

Saffron ~ ~ ~ ~ ~ ~ ~ ~ ~ ~ ~ ~ ~ ~ ~ turmeric

Drinks of The Bahamas

☀ The Bahamas offers plenty of liquid refreshment, both alcoholic and non-alcoholic. The islands are home to Kalik beer, an amber-colored drink that cools travelers on hot days. Among locals, the top drink is gin and coconut water. (Don't use coconut milk, which is much heavier.) Some sweeten the mix by adding condensed milk and jelly coconut.

Bahamian Cocktails

Yellowbird
- ½ ounce Galiano
- ½ ounce banana liqueur
- ½ ounce Tia Maria
- 1 ounce light rum
- 4 ounces pineapple juice
- 2 ounces orange juice

Mix all ingredients well. Pour over crushed ice and serve with a slice of orange or a cherry. *Serves one.* ☀

Bahama Mama
- 1¼ ounces dark rum
- 1½ ounces Nassau Royale liqueur
- 1 ounce coconut rum
- 2 ounces orange juice
- 2 ounces pineapple juice
- dash of Angostura bitters
- ⅙ ounce Grenadine

Mix all ingredients well. Pour over crushed ice and serve with a slice of orange or a cherry. *Serves one.* ☀

Planter's Punch
- 1¼ ounces gold rum
- 2 ounces orange juice
- 2 ounces pineapple juice
- dash of Angostura Bitters
- ⅙ ounce Grenadine
- 1 slice of orange (or 1 cherry)

Mix all ingredients well. Pour over crushed ice and serve
with a slice of orange or a cherry. *Serves one.* ☀

Goombay Smash, Radisson Cable Beach Resort

- *1¼ ounce dark rum*
- *1¼ ounce coconut rum*
- *4 ounces pineapple juice*

Mix all ingredients. *Serves one.* ☀

Radisson Delight, Radisson Cable Beach Resort

- *1¼ ounce blackberry brandy*
- *½ ounce banana rum*
- *2 ounces pineapple juice*
- *2 ounces cranberry juice*

Mix all ingredients. *Serves one.* ☀

Bossa Nova, Radisson Cable Beach Resort

- *½ ounce apricot brandy*
- *½ ounce Triple Sec*
- *½ ounce Galiano*
- *4 ounces pineapple juice*
- *dash of lime juice*

Mix all ingredients. *Serves one.* ☀

Cooking with Rum, by Luis Ayala

Popular around the world, Caribbean rums are usually found
as the main ingredients in a variety of exotic drinks and cocktails. The use of rum in cooking, however, is not widespread
outside the Caribbean. Just imagine how many of your favorite recipes, from savory dishes to desserts, could be magically
transported to another realm by simply adding to them a
small amount of "the nectar of the tropics."

Rum in the Caribbean is more than just a drink: very often it
is a symbol of the local culture and its heritage. For this reason, it should be easy to imagine rum as an ingredient in
many traditional dishes, beyond the popular "rum balls" and
"rum cake."

Choosing which rum to cook with can be a process as elaborate as selecting the perfect wine to accompany a meal, or as simple as looking in your rum cabinet and picking up your favorite bottle. To facilitate this process, just keep in mind that there are several types of rum, all of which will affect the recipe you are working on in a different way:

First, there are the **white rums**. These rums are typically un-aged and will have the least amount of residual flavor, especially if the recipe involves heat, which will evaporate the alcohol.

Rum punch is a popular island drink.

There are also **regular rums** and **premium rums**, which encompass most of the non-white rums in the market. Found in this category are all the **golden** and **dark/black** rums, most of which have been aged at least two years and some as much as 10 or 12 years. These rums tend to have a lot more flavor than the white rums, making recipes richer, fuller. (Most rums are aged in oak barrels previously used to age whisky. For this reason, the longer the "aging time," or the time the rum stays in the barrel, the more flavor they will develop.)

Two other categories are **spiced and flavored rums** and **over-proof** rums. In the first category you will find rums to which spices have been added during blending, with flavors such as coconut, coffee, mango, passionfruit, lemon, etc. Spiced and flavored rums tend to be sweeter than all other rums and many also have alcohol contents well below the normal 80-90° proof (40-45% alcohol by volume) found in most rums. Over-proof rums, on the other hand, are mainly White Rums whose alcohol content is that of 150 proof (75 percent) or higher.

For the purist at heart, there is still one more way of categorizing rums, one which separates them into two groups: **industrial rums** and **agricultural rums**. Industrial rums are those distilled from molasses; agricultural rums are distilled from sugarcane juice. Only rums from the French Caribbean islands are made from sugarcane juice. In these islands, both categories are indicated on the labels as either "Rhum Industrielle" or "Rhum Agricole."

A few words now about selecting the right rum for your recipe: If the intended dish will feature a complexity of subtle flavors and all you want is a hint of the tropics, use white rum. If the recipe has strong flavors that could be embellished even more, then choose a nice, rich, dark rum. For dishes already incorporating fruit elements, perhaps a dash or two of a spiced rum would do. You get the picture: have fun, experiment, and enjoy what is perhaps the world's most underrated distilled spirit today.

On The Menu

Benne seed cake. These sesame seed (called benne seeds in Africa) cakes are a favorite treat.

Chicken souse. This Bahamian soup (pronounced SOWse) is served throughout the day and made with boiled chicken, chicken giblets, onion, celery, lime, hot peppers and allspice.

Chicken Souse

- *3 pounds chicken*
- *4 cups water*
- *½ cup celery, cubed*
- *½ cup onion, diced*
- *1 pound potatoes, cubed*
- *½ cup lemon juice*
- *hot pepper sauce to taste*
- *salt and pepper to taste*

Boil chicken until cooked. Remove fat from top of water. Add vegetables and lemon juice. Bring to boil, then reduce heat to simmer for 45 minutes to one hour. Season to taste. *Serves 8-10.* ☀

Conch fritters. This tasty appetizer is a fried bread with bits of conch and seasonings. Usually served with a red dipping sauce such as cocktail sauce.

Conch Fritters

- *3 medium-size conch, chopped*
- *2 onions, chopped*
- *2 stalks celery, chopped*
- *3 tablespoons tomato paste*
- *4 cups water*
- *3 hot peppers or to taste*
- *2 tablespoons thyme*
- *4 cups flour*
- *4 tablespoons baking powder*
- *oil for frying*

Mix all ingredients except oil. Mix thoroughly and let stand 10 to 20 minutes. Heat oil in deep fryer. Scoop batter in full teaspoons, drop into hot oil. Fry until brown. *Serves 6-8.* ☀

Conch chowder. This tasty soup features local conch. (For a great conch chowder recipe, see page 116.)

Conch salad. Walk along the waterfront in Nassau and you can buy this delicious dish from any number of small stands. Why is it so popular? Besides its great taste, Bahamians swear it is an aphrodisiac. The typical conch salad is made from conch, tomatoes, onion, celery, hot peppers, lime juice and sour orange. Much like ceviche, the citrus juices cooks the sliced conch.

Cracked conch. This deep-fried entrée is a favorite lunch offering. (For another cracked conch recipe, see page 56.)

Cleaning conch on an old fishing boat.

Cracked Conch

- 2-3 medium conch
- 2 tablespoons lemon juice
- 2 tablespoons flour
- 3 eggs, beaten
- oil for frying

Prepare conch. Cut in half and flatten with mallet. Marinate in lemon juice; refrigerate for a half-hour. Remove conch from lemon juice and dip into beaten eggs then dredge in flour. Fry in skillet or deep fryer until golden brown. *Serves 3-4.* ☀

Fish and Grits. Boiled fish and grits are a favorite Bahamian breakfast dish.

Fish Tea. This spicy soup looks and tastes much better than it sounds. Watch out for fish bones when you eat this popular favorite.

Fish Tea

- *1 dozen green bananas, peeled and chopped*
- *2 onions, chopped*
- *5 pounds fresh fish, chopped*
- *1 Scotch bonnet (other hot pepper may be used to taste)*
- *Scallion to taste*
- *pepper to taste*

Boil all ingredients in a covered pot for one hour. Remove hot pepper before serving. Some cooks also add cho cho, carrots, turnips, chicken noodle soup mix and potatoes to their rendition of this soup. ❖
■ ■

Grouper. This large fish makes its appearance on just about every restaurant menu. The mild fish is served broiled, fried and just about every other imaginable way.

Guava duff. The number one Bahamian dessert is made similar to a jellyroll. Peeled and seeded guavas are rolled in a dough that has been boiled and baked. The confection is then covered with a thick sauce made from guava pulp, eggs, sugar, evaporated milk and either brandy or rum.

Johnnycake. Sometimes called journey cakes (since you could carry them along on your journey), these cakes are actually fried or baked breads. They're a favorite accompaniment to saltfish.

Peas and rice. This dish is found on just about every lunch and dinner plate in The Bahamas. (In Jamaica, this dish is known as Rice and Peas.)

Peas and Rice

- *2 cups rice*
- *1 cup peas (kidney beans or gungo peas)*

- *5 cups water*
- *1 cup pig's tail or salted beef, chopped or bacon*
- *½ teaspoon thyme*
- *½ cup diced onion*
- *½ cup green pepper, diced*
- *½ cup stewed tomatoes*
- *black pepper and salt to taste*

Boil peas until nearly tender (or used canned peas and skip this step). Add pork or salted beef. Cook for 10 minutes then add rice and remaining ingredients. Cook until rice is tender. ☀

Souse. Pronounced "SOWse", this soup is a Bahamian favorite and includes celery, peppers and meat (usually chicken, oxtail or pig's feet).

Stew fish. This stew is made with fish, celery, onions, tomatoes and plenty of spice.

Turtle soup. This thick soup features local turtle meat, cut into chunks.

Turtle steak. The green turtle makes its appearance on many island menus; its taste is similar to veal.

☼ What To Eat, When

If you are a hesitant eater, have no fear: you will find traditional American breakfasts and other meals served at every resort on the island. However, when you're ready to give your taste buds a holiday as well, look to the Bahamian dishes for a pick-me-up. Here's a look at traditional foods found in local restaurants and homes.

BREAKFAST: Boiled fish and johnnycake; fish 'n grits.

LUNCH: Cracked conch or conch salad; peas and rice.

DINNER: Bahamian lobster; peas and rice; baked breadfruit; guava duff.

The Bahamas

Regional Delights

Throughout this section, we'll take a look at travel in The Bahamas' various islands, from bustling Nassau and Freeport to quiet Bimini and tranquil Harbour Island.

Each section highlights what the traveler needs to know to plan a trip that's as satisfying as it is savory. We'll take a look at recommended restaurants, with information on what makes each unique. These eateries cover a full spectrum of dining styles, from white glove service in elegant restaurants to roadside joints where lunch will be handed to you sans plate, fork, or napkin.

Following recommended restaurants, we'll list some additional restaurants found in each region, good eateries that, because of lack of space, aren't explored in depth but give you some options to make your own discoveries. Throughout this section, we'll sprinkle in recommendations by fellow travelers who have made their own discoveries.

Where you stay also has a strong influence on where you eat, especially if you select an all-inclusive resort. To help you make the right decisions on where you should stay, we've included sections on accommodations of all types, from luxurious all-inclusives to intimate inns. We've listed the amenities at each of these properties and have provided information on dining options, especially important when selecting an all-inclusive property. While you may be dining three times a day, man cannot live by bread (or breadfruit) alone, so we've included a *Between Meals* section for each region. Whether your idea of a good time means climbing a stair-stepped waterfall, seeking out a secluded beach, touring historic plantation houses, or checking out the local museums, we'll point you in the right direction.

The islands of The Bahamas boast a wide variety of sporting activities, both on land and on water. World-class golfing, challenging hikes, tennis with instruction by resident pros, scuba diving, deep-sea fishing, and adventurous bicycle trips are found across the islands. To introduce you to these sporting activities, we've included *Work off Those Meals* sections for each region to give you plenty of activities, no matter how much you've over-indulged at that buffet.

Finally, since all good things must come to an end, you'll want to take home a taste of The Bahamas at the end of your journey. In the *Shopping* section, we've included shops, grocery stores, markets, and boutiques where you can find rums, marinades, sauces, jellies, and just about every other kind of food product to make your taste of the islands last a little longer. We've also included mail order options in the *Appendix*.

Choosing A Destination

☀ OK, now the tough part: which area of The Bahamas do you choose? The decision will be based on several factors. Ask yourself some questions to help determine what you want.

- ☀ What type of destination are you looking for: quiet, action-packed, cultural?
- ☀ How long is your vacation? If you are on a three-night package, stick to Nassau or Freeport or you'll lose a lot of time in transit to the Out Islands.

Here's a rundown of the major destinations:

Abaco Islands

Population: 10,000
Area: 650 square miles

This chain is nicknamed the "Top of the Bahamas" and is a popular destination with sailors. The Abacos are noted for their New England architecture, a reminder of the founders who came to the region after the American Revolution.

The Acklins and Crooked Island

Population: 412
Area: 92 square miles

These southern islands, divided only by a narrow passage, are little explored and home to just small villages. Remote beaches and good bonefishing draw visitors.

Andros Islands

Population: 8,180
Area: 2,300 square miles

These islands are known for their gamefishing. Andros is the largest Bahamian island and is often called the "Bonefishing Capital of the World." The island is also located on the fringe of the third largest barrier reef in the world, making it a popular destination for scuba divers.

The Berry Islands

Population: 700
Area: 12 square miles

The small Berries are popular with yachties, anglers, and divers.

Bimini Islands

Population: 1,600
Area: 9 square miles

Best known as just "Bimini," these islands are tops with sportsfishermen and are known as the "Big Gamefishing Capital of the Globe." Once the roost of writer Ernest Hemingway.

Cat Island

Population: 1,698
Area: 150 square miles

This 50-mile-long island is thought by many to be one of the prettiest in The Bahamas thanks to its pink sand beaches and rolling hills (including the highest point in the Bahamas).

Eleuthera/Harbour Island

Population: 10,600
Area: 200 square miles

Skinny Eleuthera is under three miles wide but packs a lot of activity in its reaches. The island is especially known for its pineapples. Harbour Island, a short ferry ride away, sports New England architecture and pink sand beaches. A favorite with yachties and snorkelers who find good snorkeling just offshore.

The Exumas

Population: 4,000
Area: 112 square miles

This chain consists of 365 cays and islands, making it a popular boating destination.

Grand Bahama Island

Population: 50,000
Area: 530 square miles

The second most-visited island in The Bahamas, this island is home to Freeport, the country's second largest city. Snorkelers, scuba divers, golfers, shoppers, and more find plenty of diversions here.

Long Island

Population: 2,954
Area: 173 square miles

Seventy-six miles long, Long Island is known for its beautiful beaches.

New Providence Island

Population: 171,542
Area: 80 square miles

Home of Nassau and Paradise Island, this is the hub of the Bahamian tourism industry. Around-the-clock action in the form of casinos and live shows fill evenings, while daytime fun can include everything from golf to scuba diving to duty-free shopping.

San Salvador and Rum Cay

Population: 465
Area: 63 square miles

The island – where Christopher Columbus first landed in The Bahamas – is still remote and quiet, with most residents living off farming or fishing.

☼ How Much Will It Cost?

Restaurant Dining

If you see a restaurant designated "All-Inclusive" in the price listing, this is a restaurant in an all-inclusive resort. Guests at the resort can dine at the restaurant as part of their package. But what if you're not staying at the resort?

Have no fear. We've included the local telephone number of the resort, so just give them a call and ask about purchasing a day pass. Most Bahamian all-inclusives sell both day and evening passes for the resorts which allow non-guests to come on property and enjoy the hospitality. Everyone comes out a winner. You get to try a new restaurant and the resort gets to tempt you with delights in the hope that you might want to book your next vacation there.

In general, restaurants throughout The Bahamas tend to price out as follows:

Cost of a Meal Per Person

In US dollars, excluding drinks and tip

$$$$ - *over $30*
$$$ - *$21-$30*
$$ - *$10-$20*
$ - *Under $10*

A Hotel Stay

Here's a price breakdown for a standard room, based on double occupancy in high season under an EP (room-only) plan:

Cost of Accommodations Per Person

In US dollars

$$$$- *over $300*
$$$- *$201-$300*
$$- *$101-$200*
$ - *under $100*

For an all-inclusive, where meals, drinks, tips, transportation, and sometimes even more is included, prices are given per person for adults, based on double occupancy.

The Abacos

Sailors and yachties are well acquainted with the Abacos, the family of island located 106 miles north of Nassau or 175 miles east of Palm Beach. The island chain spans 650 square miles in the northeastern end of The Bahamas. They are so far north, in fact, that they are often called "The Top of the Bahamas."

The Islands are the second largest island group in The Bahamas, with developed islands that include Great Abaco, Elbow Cay, Man-O-War Cay, Great Guana Cay, Treasure Cay, Green Turtle Cay, Spanish Cay, and Walker Cay. Great Abaco is located on the western side of the island group, separated by the Sea of Abaco from the cays on the east.

History

The history of these islands is interesting. After the American Revolution, disenchanted British Loyalists moved here from New England and the Carolinas, bringing with them New England building styles. They also brought with them boat-building skills – and soon adapted those skills to include pirating. On Abaco's ocean floor rest nearly 500 Spanish galleons.

Today that pirate legacy has resulted in many good scuba diving sites, including Devil's Hole, eight miles north of Treasure Cay, and the Pelican Cay National Park, between Lynyard Cay and Tilloo Cay south of Marsh Harbour, a 2,000-acre land and sea park. The pirating days came to an end in the mid-1800s when the Abaconians built the first lighthouses.

The Bahamas

Descendants of those early residents never forgot their ties to the Mother Country. In 1972, when The Bahamas asked for independence from Britain, the Abaconians petitioned Queen Elizabeth II to allow their islands to remain a British colony. The petition was not granted.

Getaways

Today the Abacos offer a variety of getaways for the traveler, including near-deserted islands and bustling towns.

ELBOW CAY. Five miles east of Marsh Harbour lies Elbow Cay. The community of Hope Town overlooks the harbor and is filled with pastel houses built in a New England style. You can't miss the candy-striped lighthouse erected in 1863. Today it is one of the few manned lighthouses in The Bahamas.

GREAT ABACO. This large island is home to Marsh Harbour, third largest city in The Bahamas. Here visitors will find plenty of shopping, nightlife, dining, and watersports fun. Marsh Harbour is a good base from which to plan trips to neighboring cays, offering regular ferry service to Hope Town in Elbow Cay and to Man-O-War Cay. It's one of the biggest yachting centers in the Bahamas and has a fun, yachty atmosphere.

GREAT GUANA CAY. Located 10 miles from Marsh Harbour by boat, this laid-back island is noted for its beautiful beaches, an excellent offshore reef, and good watersports.

GREEN TURTLE CAY. One of the oldest settlements in the Abacos, Green Turtle Cay is home to New Plymouth, a colonial village that looks like something right out of a time warp. New England-style buildings dot the island's southern tip, a reminder of those early British Loyalists who relocated here. Green Turtle Cay is located just east of Treasure Cay and is popular with those looking for watersports, gamefishing, and bonefishing.

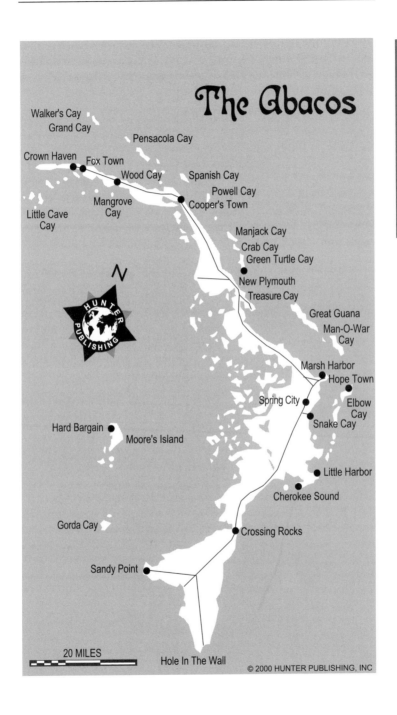

The Abacos

Walker's Cay
Grand Cay

Pensacola Cay

Crown Haven · Fox Town

Wood Cay

Spanish Cay

Powell Cay
Cooper's Town

Mangrove Cay

Little Cave Cay

N

HUNTER PUBLISHING

Manjack Cay

Crab Cay
Green Turtle Cay

New Plymouth
Treasure Cay

Great Guana
Man-O-War Cay

Marsh Harbor
Hope Town

Spring City

Elbow Cay

Snake Cay

Hard Bargain

Moore's Island

Little Harbor

Cherokee Sound

Gorda Cay

Crossing Rocks

Sandy Point

20 MILES

Hole In The Wall

© 2000 HUNTER PUBLISHING, INC

The Bahamas

LITTLE HARBOUR. This charming cay was once accessible only by boat, but today you can come via road from Marsh Harbour. Diving, snorkeling, shelling and cave exploring are all found here.

MAN-O-WAR CAY. From Marsh Harbour take a ferry out to Man-O-War Cay, the top boat-building area in the Abacos. Not only do large boats and yachts come to this region known as the nautical capital of the Abacos, collectors also venture to Man-O-War Cay to visit Joe Albury. For generations, Albury's family has crafted sailing dinghies and gifts in the studio, all crafted from Abaco hardwoods. The atmosphere on Man-O-War is very family oriented. it maintains a more formal dress style and there are no liquor stores.

SPANISH CAY. Spanish Cay is popular with anglers and divers.

TREASURE CAY. Accessible by boat or automobile from Marsh Harbour, Treasure Cay is the second most populated area on Great Abaco. The cay is home to the only 18-hole championship golf course in the Abacos. The island includes condominiums, resorts, and visitor facilities.

WALKER'S CAY. This ritzy island has been featured in many publications and is a favorite with anglers, divers, and yachties.

Recommended
Restaurants

ABACO INN RESTAURANT, $$-$$$
Hope Town, Elbow Cay
☎ *242/366-0133*
Dress code: Casually elegant
Reservations: required

☀Gourmet dining with both Bahamian and international dishes is the order of the day at this excellent restaurant.

Diners enjoy a view of the beach and the gentle surf. With candlelit tables, this makes a romantic spot for dinner. Specialties include lamb chops and blackened fish. Open for breakfast, lunch, and dinner. On most Saturday and Sunday evenings the restaurant showcases local entertainers.

ANGLER'S RESTAURANT, $$-$$$
Abaco Beach Resort & Boat Harbour
☎ *242/367-2871*
Dress code: casually elegant
Reservations: recommended

This waterside restaurant overlooks Boat Harbour marina and serves international cuisine with an island flair. Breakfast offers traditional bacon and egg dishes as well as Belgian waffles, French toast, corned beef hash, and smoked salmon. Lunch choices include chicken wings with blue cheese dip, coconut-mango shrimp with fruit chutney and conch fritters. Linen tablecloths and candles provide an elegant flair at dinnertime. The evening menu features dishes such as fresh shrimp, group and scallops tossed with red or white sauce and creamy risotto, an island seafood cake with grilled shrimp sparked by avocado chutney, and sushi prepared using the day's catch.

A tempting feast at the Angler's Restaurant.

Oven-Roasted Grouper Fillet with Veggies, Abaco Beach Resort

Grouper:

- *4 pieces fresh grouper, each 6-7 ounces, filleted and skinned*
- *6-8 cloves garlic, minced*
- *2 ounces shallots, mined*
- *2 ounces fresh cilantro, finely chopped*
- *1 ounce white peppercorns, freshly ground*
- *3 ounces olive oil*
- *1 whole lime, juiced*

Combine shallots, garlic, cilantro, peppercorns, and olive oil. Brush mixture on grouper filets and season with lime juice and salt. Saute in frying pan, and roast until tender in oven. ☀

Sweet Potato Cakes:

- *½ pound sweet potatoes, peeled and boiled*
- *4 ounces butter*
- *4 egg yolks*
- *1 cup all-purpose flour*
- *salt to taste*
- *freshly ground pepper to taste*
- *nutmeg to taste*

Press boiled potatoes through a sieve or potato ricer. Combine potatoes, butter, egg yolks, seasonings, and flour to form a soft dough ball. Roll into 2-inch cylinder and cut into ½-inch pieces. Fry in non-stick pan until golden brown on each side. ☀

Grilled Zucchini:

- *12 ounces zucchini, sliced*
- *3 ounces olive oil*
- *4-6 cloves garlic, minced*
- *fresh basil to taste*
- *freshly ground black pepper to taste*

Combine ingredients and grill. ☀

Warm Pineapple Salsa:

- *1 ounce olive oil*
- *½ ounce shallots, minced*
- *1 jalapeño pepper, peeled, seeded, and minced*

- *½ ounce fresh ginger, minced*
- *8 ounces fresh pineapple, diced*
- *5 ounces fresh orange juice*
- *½ tablespoon fresh mint, finely chopped*
- *½ tablespoon fresh basil, finely chopped*
- *1-2 tablespoon fresh cilantro, finely chopped*
- *salt to taste*

Heat the oil and add the pepper, shallots and ginger. Sauté until the aroma is released. Add the orange juice and reduce slightly. Add the pineapple and herbs and warm gently. Do not allow the salsa to simmer.

Pool the salsa on each individual plate; center with the grouper and drizzle more salsa on top. Arrange the zucchini and sweet potatoes on the side. *Yields four servings.*

Chef's Tip: Chef Dietmar Viberreiter recommends wearing rubber gloves to peel, seed and mince the jalapeño peppers. ☀

Chef Profile: Angler's Restaurant highlights the work of Executive Chef **Dietmar Viberreiter.** *The Austrian chef was educated in Switzerland and has worked in Bermuda, St. Lucia and, most recently, as a private chef in Lyford Cay.*

BJ'S RESTAURANT AND BAR, $
Mount Hope, Little Abaco
☎ 242 / 365-2205
Dress code: casual
Reservations: not required

This local diner serves Bahamian dishes in a casual atmosphere. There's nothing fancy about the setting; people come here for the food. Breakfast starts the day rolling here with local favorites such as boiled fish with johnnycake, chicken souse, eggs and grits, or French toast. The lunch menu adds burgers and sandwiches.

h, fried or steamed chicken, steamed turtle, ers, barbecued ribs, steamed fish, curried beef ribs are a few favorites on the dinner menu. hours bring plenty of action with live entertain-ncing.

BLUFF HOUSE RESTAURANT, $$$
Green Turtle Cay, ☎ 242/365-4247
Dress code: dressy
Reservations: required

Gourmet dinners served under the soft glow of candles are served in the historic main house. Recently renovated to its historic splendor, the restaurant offers up to five entrée selections every night from 7:30pm. Breakfast is served in the restaurant as well as outdoors on the patio by the pool.

Popular dinner entrées include Bahamian grouper fillet coated in a tomato and basil sauce and topped with melted mozzarella cheese; crispy duck breast served with a grapefruit and Grand Marnier sauce; filet mignon Forestier served with a mushroom, bacon and parsley sauce; Bahamian lobster tail with a special lemon and butter sauce; and roast loin of lamb wrapped in bacon and served with a honey and rosemary glaze.

Bluff House Grouper, Bluff House Restaurant

- *1 pound boneless grouper fillet*
- *½ cup virgin olive oil*
- *2 cloves garlic, finely chopped*
- *2 large tomatoes, finely chopped*
- *2 teaspoons fresh basil*
- *2 shallots, finely chopped*
- *½ cup white wine*
- *mozzarella cheese*

Mince garlic and combine with olive oil. Add the grouper fillet. Allow to marinate for at least one hour. Place the shallots in a hot pan with a teaspoon of butter and cook on low heat until soft. Add tomatoes, basil, and wine and cook for another 15 minutes on low heat. Remove the sauce from heat.

Remove the grouper fillet from the marinade and place in hot frying pan. When the fish is cooked, coat with tomato sauce, top with mozzarella and place under a grill or in an oven until cheese is melted. *Yields two servings.* ☀

■ ■

CAP'N JACK'S, $-$$
Hope Town, ☎ *242 / 366-0247*
Dress code: casual
Reservations: optional

Located right on the harbor, this Cap'n Jacks offers Bahamian dishes in the casual atmosphere of what looks like a large, white house. Enjoy grilled grouper, crawfish salad, conch plate, or a steak sandwich with sautéed mushrooms and onions. Kid's meals and sandwiches are available. Every night except Sunday you can enjoy a special dinner with offerings such as lamb chops, New York strip steak, fried shrimp, Cornish game hen, and more. Live music keeps the action moving Wednesdays and Fridays and happy hour packs the bar from 5 to 6:30 each night. If you're coming in by boat, you can radio in on VHF Channel 16 for reservations.

MAVIS COUNTRY RESTAURANT, $
Don McKay Boulevard, Marsh Harbour
☎ *242 / 367-2002 or 2050*
Dress code: casual
Reservations: not required

Located just south of the traffic light in downtown Marsh Harbour, this charming little eatery offers a real taste of Bahamian and Jamaican food with good service and good prices to match. Some favorite dishes include native grouper or snapper; chicken either steamed, barbecued, fried or baked; barbecued ribs; stewed beef; lamb chops; curried goat; curried chicken; ackee and saltfish; jerk chicken; and steamed oxtail. Vegetarian dishes, burgers, and sandwiches are also offered. You'll probably have the chance to meet the owner and cook, Mavis Reckley, and might be served by one of her two daughters. Take-out orders are also available.

NIPPERS BAR AND GRILL, $$
Great Guana Cay, ☎ *242/365-5143*
Dress code: casual
Reservations: suggested

☀This restaurant is perched on the edge of a bluff and offers a wonderful view of the world's third largest barrier reef. Open for lunch and dinner, Nippers features local specialties, as well as a pig roast on Sundays.

THE PALMS BEACH CLUB AND BAR, $-$$
Green Turtle Cay, ☎ *242/365-4247*
Dress code: casual
Reservations: not required

☀This casual eatery is part of Bluff House and offers a casual alternative for lunch. Local specialties are especially wonderful, such as the cracked conch (recipe below).

Bluff House Cracked Conch, Bluff House

- *4 conch, well pounded*
- *½ cup milk*
- *1 cup seasoned flour*
- *cooking oil*
- *salt and pepper*
- *Tabasco*
- *¼ cup lime juice*

Marinate conch in lime juice, drain. Dip into milk and then dredge in seasoned flour. Cover bottom of heavy pan with oil, fry conch over medium heat, covered. Season to taste. Optional: fry slowly in butter with dried onions, omit oil. *Serves four.* ☀

THE SPINNAKER RESTAURANT, $$-$$$
Treasure Cay, ☎ *242/365-8469*
Dress code: casual
Reservations: suggested

☀Breakfast, lunch and dinner are served at this eatery. Lunch visitors can enjoy Bahamian fried fish, a spicy concoction, while evening guests can select from gourmet items such as duck à l'orange and filet mignon bearnaise. Like the island itself, the atmosphere here is fun. Dinner at the Spinnaker is a good way to end your island day.

Where To Stay

ABACO BEACH RESORT & BOAT HARBOUR MARINA, $$
Marsh Harbour, ☎ 800/468-4799, 242/367-2158
E-mail: abrandbh@batelnet.bs; www.greatabacobeach.com

This resort offers 52 oceanfront rooms and six private two-bedroom cottages, each with either private terraces or oceanview balconies. Each room has mini refrigerator, air-conditioning, wet bar, coffee maker, satellite TV, hair dryer and, in the cottages, a full kitchen.

Other amenities include a dive site, grocery store, liquor store, and a 180-slip marina, the largest in The Bahamas. The marina caters to vessels up to 200 feet long and has cable TV and telephone hookups for the largest slips. Guests also enjoy a private beach, two pools (including a swim-up bar), tennis, bicycle rentals, and the Angler's Restaurant.

Island culinary delights are served at the Angler's Restaurant.

Curry Plantain Soup, Abaco Beach Resort

- *1½ ounces onions or shallots, diced*
- *10 stalks celery, diced*
- *1½ cloves garlic, minced*
- *1 ounce vegetable oil*
- *1 tablespoon sugar*
- *1 tablespoon cider vinegar*
- *2 tablespoons curry powder*
- *1 pound (about six) plantains, peeled and diced*
- *1 quart chicken stock*
- *2 ounces heavy cream*
- *⅛ teaspoon nutmeg*
- *½ teaspoon ginger*
- *5 teaspoons cilantro, chopped*
- *salt and pepper to taste*

Heat oil in large pan. Add shallots, celery, garlic, nutmeg and ginger and sauté until golden brown. Stir in sugar and caramelize lightly. Add curry powder and plantains and mix well. Add chicken stock and bring to a boil, allowing to simmer for 20 minutes. Add heavy cream and simmer for 10 minutes more. Remove from heat and blend soup until texture is smooth. Sprinkle with chopped cilantro and season with salt and pepper. *Serves five.* ☀

BANYAN BEACH CLUB, $$-$$$
Treasure Cay
☎ *888/625-3060, 242/365-8111, fax 365-8226*
www.banyanbeach.com

Two- and three-bedroom condominiums are offered by this beachside hideaway. They're located on "one of the 10 best beaches in the world," according to *National Geographic.* When you've had your fill of strolling that white sand beach, tennis, golf, scuba, fishing, and shopping are found nearby.

BLUFF HOUSE CLUB AND MARINA, $-$$$$$
Green Turtle Cay
☎ *242/365-4257, fax 365-4248*
E-mail: bluffhouse@oii.net; www.oii.net/BluffHouse

☀ The Bluff House offers true upscale elegance in its 28 guest rooms and villas. All rooms include refrigerators, coffee makers, and hair dryers. The resort also has an excellent gourmet eatery.

Bluff House Tranquil Turtle

☀ This drink has greeted many guests at the Main House Bar. The recipe makes a gallon jug.

- *jigger of vodka*
- *jigger of gin*
- *jigger of grenadine*
- *jigger of whisky*
- *jigger of coconut rum*
- *jigger of banana rum*
- *46 ounces orange juice*
- *46 ounces pineapple juice*
- *6 jiggers of white rum*
- *6 jiggers of dark rum*
- *top up with 151 Rum*

Mix the juices in a gallon jug. Add other ingredients and shake and pour. ☀

COCO BAY COTTAGES, $$-$$$
P.O. Box AB-795, Green Turtle Cay
☎ *800/752-0166, 242/365-5464, fax 365-5465*
E-mail: cocobay@oii.net; www.oii.net/cocobay

☀ Four two- and-three bedroom cottages make up this quiet hideaway that's a favorite with those who enjoy bonefishing, snorkeling, and diving. This casual getaway is a good choice for those who want to make their own fun.

CONCH INN MARINA AND HOTEL, $
Marsh Harbour, Great Abaco
☎ 800/688-4752, 242/367-4000, fax 367-4004

☀This small hotel has just nine rooms. It's adjacent to one of the area's best marinas. Operated by The Moorings, the largest charter yacht company in the world, Conch Inn Marina is often used by those yachties coming to charter a vessel either the night of their arrival or the night before their departure. Rooms include cable TV and air-conditioning as well as access to a freshwater pool.

HOPE TOWN HIDEAWAYS LTD., $$
Hope Town, Elbow Cay
☎ *800 / 688-4752, 242 / 365-0224, fax 366-0434*
www.hopetown.com

☀These villas have all the comforts of home: telephone, air-conditioning, and a full kitchen. There's even a private dock.

TREASURE CAY HOTEL RESORT AND MARINA, $$
Treasure Cay
☎ 800/327-1584, 957/525-7711, fax 954/525-1699
E-mail: abaco@gate.net; www.treasurecay.com

☀Golfers will appreciate this beachside resort, home to an 18-hole, par 72 championship golf course was designed by Dick Wilson. The resort also boasts a 150-slip marina and is located on an incredible white sand beach. Other amenities include tennis, a freshwater pool, dive shop, bicycle rentals, and more.

Between Meals

Albert Lowe Museum
Main Street, Marsh Harbour
☎ *242 / 365-4049*
Hours: weekdays, call for hours
Admission: donation

This museum showcases the history of the Abacos and its shipbuilding traditions. It was founded by Alton Lowe in memory of his father, a well-known ship-model craftsman.

People-to-People
☎ *242/326-5371, 242/328-7810, 242/356-0435-8*
Admission: free, except for cost of any activities
The People-to-People program is an excellent way to learn more about Bahamian residents and culture. This program matches vacationers with more than 1,500 Bahamian volunteers for a day of activities that might include shopping at a local market, dinner with a local family, fishing, boating, or a tour of backstreet sights.

Wyannie Malone Historical Museum
Hope Town, Elbow Cay
☎ *242/366-0033*
Hours: Sunday to Friday, 11-3, Saturday, 10:30-2:30
Admission: small fee
This small museum is filled with the rich history of this island.

Working Off Those Meals

⁂ Golf

An 18-hole golf course designed by Dick Wilson is found a half-mile from Treasure Cay Resort and Marina. The course is par 72, 6,985 yards, and is a great choice for golfers who want to take a break from the crowds. For information call ☎ 800/327-1584 or 954/525-7711.

⁂ Snorkeling & Diving

Several dive operators operate on Andros. Check with **Dive Abaco** in Marsh Harbor for all types of trips ranging from

snorkel excursions to night, shark and wreck dives. Call
☎ 800/247-5338 or 242/247-5338.

Turtles

*Green Turtle Cay is home to, quite predictably,
green turtles. These are bred on farms as a food
source and you'll find turtle soup and stew on several local menus. You'll also find products made
from turtle shells in some local stores. Note, however, that importation of these turtle products in the
US is illegal (even for international passengers in
transit through the US). If you purchase any of these
goods, they will be confiscated by US Customs.*

Andros

If you've ever flown from Miami to the Caribbean, you
probably flew right over Andros. There's no way to miss
this giant island; it spans 2,300 square miles and is one of the
largest tracts of unexplored land in the Western Hemisphere.

Andros is easy to spot from the air because it splinters like a
waterlogged chunk of land floating in the sea. The island is
home to many lakes and inlets, each favorites with
bonefishermen. Along its fringes, snorkelers and scuba divers
find some of the best activity in the area, thanks to the third
largest barrier island in the world just offshore.

"Andros may be one of our best kept secrets," says Vincent
Vanderpool-Wallace, Director General of the Ministry of
Tourism. "With its peaceful villages and spectacular, un-
spoiled scenery, it's the perfect destination for those who really want to get away from it all. Yet, it's quick and easy to
reach for US vacationers."

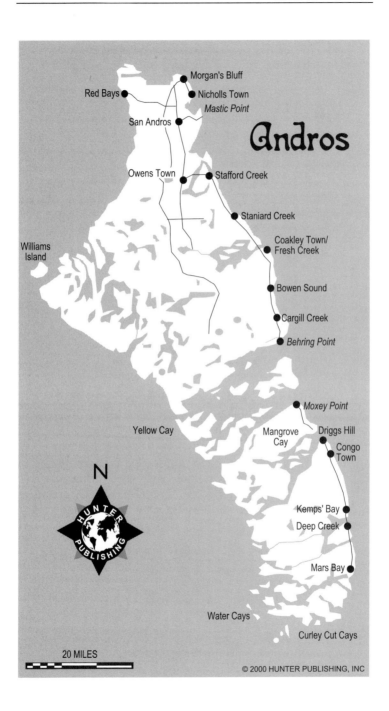

Gndros

Morgan's Bluff
Red Bays
Nicholls Town
Mastic Point
San Andros
Owens Town
Stafford Creek
Staniard Creek
Coakley Town/
Fresh Creek
Williams
Island
Bowen Sound
Cargill Creek
Behring Point
Moxey Point
Yellow Cay
Mangrove
Cay
Driggs Hill
Congo
Town
Kemps' Bay
Deep Creek
Mars Bay
Water Cays
Curley Cut Cays
N
HUNTER PUBLISHING
20 MILES
© 2000 HUNTER PUBLISHING, INC

The Bahamas

Chickcharnies and Luscas

Andros is the home of the legendary Chickcharnies. These three-toed, red-eyed elves sport beards and feathers and supposedly live deep in the island. The tale of these impish beasts has thrived here for generations, scaring young children and explaining away odd occurrences.

The Chickcharnies are not alone on Andros, however. This island is also home to the Luscas, said to resemble octopus. These evil spirits supposedly live in dark blue holes in the sea. Whenever their domain is threatened, the Luscas drag men and their boats to their death.

Recommended Restaurants

ANDROS ISLAND BONEFISHING CLUB, $$
Cargill Creek, ☎ 242/368-5167
Dress code: casual
Reservations: suggested

Bahamian fare is the order of the day at this restaurant, starting with Bahamian pancakes for breakfast and continuing to dishes such as baked lobster, grouper, and peas and rice for lunch and dinner. Bring your best fish tale to share at this casual eatery!

SMALL HOPE BAY LODGE, $$
Fresh Creek, ☎ 242/368-2013
Dress code: casually elegant
Reservations: suggested

The lodge offers an American-style breakfast and, for lunch, a buffet. Local seafood, including lobster and conch, are the specialties for the evening meal, which always includes a meat or fish dish as well as a salad bar, fresh vegetables and dessert bar. The family-friendly restaurant is a fun place to end a day at the beach.

TRANQUILITY HILL RESTAURANT, $-$$
Behring Point, ☎ *242/368-4132*
Dress code: casual
Reservations: suggested

Bahamian cuisine draws diners to this small eatery which serves up conch, grouper, snapper, crawfish, and chowder in a relaxed, casual atmosphere.

Where To Stay

ANDROS ISLAND BONEFISHING CLUB, $$
Cargill Creek
☎ *800/688-4752, 242/368-5167, fax 368-5235*

This small hotel is, as the name suggests, a favorite with the bonefishing crowd. Guides are available for a day of fishing on the flats and the hotel even has a fly-tying table for those hours off the water. Twelve rooms are offered here and the hotel includes a good restaurant (see above).

ANDROS LIGHTHOUSE YACHT CLUB & MARINA, $$
Fresh Creek
☎ *800/688-4752, 242/368-2305, fax 368-2300*

Twelve guest rooms here are located alongside the 18-slip marina. The causal-style rooms are bright, decorated in island tones. They have cool tile floors, television and air-conditioning. There's also a freshwater pool.

EMERALD PALMS BY-THE-SEA, $$
Driggs Hill, South Andros
☎ *800/688-4752, 242/368-2661, fax 368-2667*

This beachside guest accommodation is just steps from the water and the nearby coral reef. All guest rooms include air-conditioning, ceiling fans, refrigerator and televisions.

SMALL HOPE BAY LODGE, $$
Fresh Creek
☎ *800/223-6961, 242/368-2013 or 2014,*
954/927-7096, fax 242/368-2015
E-mail: shbmkt@smallhope.com; www.SmallHope.com

⁖☀⁖A favorite with scuba divers, this lodge holds the title as one of the oldest hotels in the Bahamas, dating back to 1960. Guests can select from 20 one- and two-bedroom cottages on the beach, each decorated in a local style and built of native coral rocks. The all-inclusive rate here covers all meals, drinks, airport transfers, and use of snorkeling equipment, bicycles, sailboats, kayaks, and windsurfers. Dive packages are available with three dives a day. Non-guests can come by to enjoy the restaurant.

TRANQUILITY HILL BONEFISH LODGE, $$
Behring Point
☎ *800/688-4752, 242/368-4132, fax 368-4132*
E-mail: tranquility@batelnet.bs

⁖☀⁖Anglers hold this resort near to their hearts thanks to the on-site fishing guides with 16-foot skiffs. Guides specialize in bonefishing, although shark and deep-sea fishing excursions can also be arranged.

Working Off Those Meals

⁙ Scuba Diving

As home of the largest **coral reef** in the Western Hemisphere and the third largest in the world, it's no surprise that this is a favorite destination with scuba divers. Waters start shallow on the reef, just six to 15 feet, but drop to inky black depths at the Tongue of the Ocean, a deepwater trench.

The waters surrounding these islands are also dotted with shipwrecks. The **Lady Gloria**, a mailboat sunk off Morgan's Bluff, and the **Potomac**, a steel-hulled barge that now is filled with grouper, parrot fish, and barracuda, are two favorite sites with divers.

The Berry Islands

This family of islands made up of over 30 islands and cays (many privately owned) is largely uninhabited. Sprinkled in the ocean like a chain of pearls, the Berry Islands are 150 miles east of Miami and 35 miles north of Nassau. These quiet islands are a favorite spot for gamefishing. Serious anglers come here to try their luck at a marlin, sailfish, or mackerel.

Recommended Restaurants

THE BEACH CLUB, $
Great Harbour Cay, ☎ 242/367-8838
Dress code: casual
Reservations: not required

This restaurant serves breakfast and lunch as well as cocktails until 6 pm. Located at Great Harbour Cay Yacht Club, this relaxed place is a favorite spot for chatting and sharing stories.

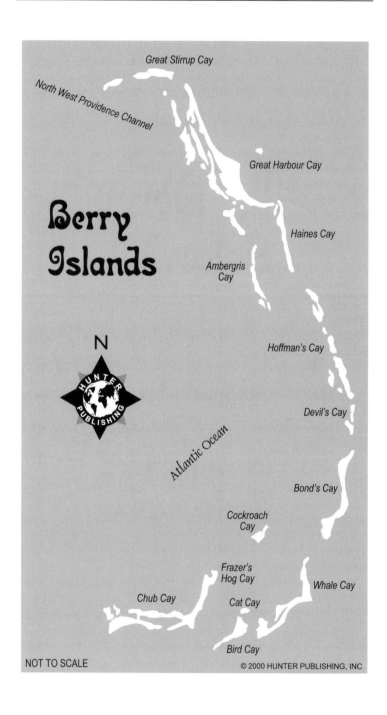

Great Stirrup Cay

North West Providence Channel

Great Harbour Cay

Berry Islands

Haines Cay

Ambergris Cay

N

Hoffman's Cay

Devil's Cay

Atlantic Ocean

Bond's Cay

Cockroach Cay

Frazer's Hog Cay

Whale Cay

Chub Cay

Cat Cay

Bird Cay

NOT TO SCALE

© 2000 HUNTER PUBLISHING, INC

TAMBOO DINNER CLUB, $$-$$$
Great Harbour Cay, ☎ *242/367-8838*
Dress code: casual, casually elegant
Reservations: required

This restaurant is open for dinner only and serves a variety of continental and Bahamian dishes. It's right on the waterfront, and is a popular place with beachgoers at the end of the day.

Where To Stay

GREAT HARBOUR CAY
YACHT CLUB AND MARINA, $$-$$$
Great Harbour Cay
☎ *800/343-7256, 242/367-8838, fax 367-8115*

Great Harbour Cay is a private island and home to villas and two-bedroom townhouses. Rooms have full kitchens, air-conditioning and linens, as well as maid service. An 80-slip marina is located here as well.

Working Off Those Meals

☸ Scuba Diving

One of the top dive sites is **Mamma Rhoda Rock**. This 16-foot dive along the coral reef is home to many crawfish and moray eels. Hoffman Cay's **blue hole**, 600 feet deep, is another popular site.

The Bimini Islands

☀ Just 50 mile east of Miami lie the Biminis, a chain of islands and cays closer than any other to the US. You often hear "Bimini" as a single destination, but travelers should set their course for **North Bimini, South Bimini** or one of the other many cays such as **Gun Cay, Ocean Cay** or the ritzy private island of **Cat Cay.**

The Hemingway Connection

If you've heard of the Biminis, it is probably due to Ernest Hemingway, undoubtedly the most famous Bimini booster. The writer came to these islands to write Islands in the Stream *and* To Have and Have Not *as well as to fish, swap fish tales, and down a few cold ones at The Compleat Angler bar.*

Today Ernest's seat at the bar has been taken over by any number of other gamefishermen, who come from around the globe to test their skills in what is often called the gamefishing capital of the world. Here records are set for trophy sailfish, tuna, and wahoo.

The largest destination in this chain is North Bimini, just about 7½ miles long. The major community is Alice Town.

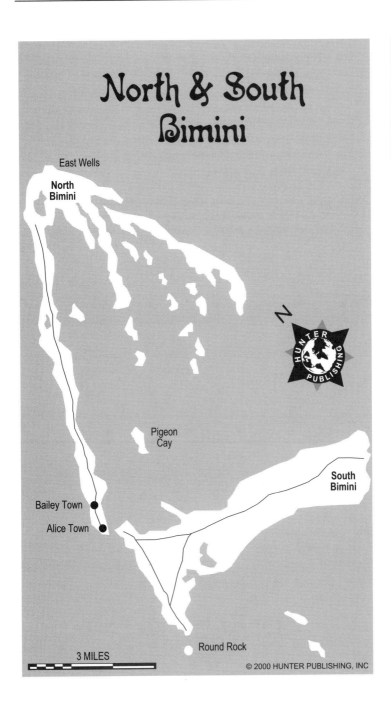

History

The Biminis have a rich history that continues to interest many people, especially those with an eye for mystery. These islands are home to four mystical sites:

The Lost City of Atlantis

Yes, rumor has it that the Lost City of Atlantis just might have been found. Researchers began the task of studying large stones that appear to be part of an underground road, which would date this region to 10,000 B.C. When you fly over the Biminis, this Bimini Road is easy to see from the air.

Sand Mounds

Researchers are puzzled by large sand mounds in the shape of a shark, cat, and a sea horse that lie in North Bimini. These are so huge their shapes can be seen only from the air. Just so you don't think that these were the work of some trickster, know that the mounds appear on early maps of the island – maps drawn at a time when there was no air travel.

The Fountain of Youth

Ponce DeLeon came to the Biminis in 1513 in search of the elusive fountain. Supposedly the explorer was given directions by the local Indians and told to search for it in a place called BeeMeeNee.

The Healing Hole

A labyrinth of narrow tunnels lies north of Bimini. One of these tunnels is connected to a creek that is called The Healing Hole. At high tide, the tunnels fill with water and empty into the creek. The waters, which are high in mineral content, are said to have healing powers.

Recommended Restaurants

THE ANCHORAGE, $$
Bimini Blue Water, Alice Town
☎ 242/347-3066
Dress code: casual
Reservations: suggested

This oceanside restaurant is open for lunch and dinner. It's nothing fancy, but does offer tasty Bahamian dishes featuring fresh catches and just-baked bread.

THE COMPLEAT ANGLER, $
Alice Town, ☎ 242/347-3391
Dress code: casual
Reservations: not required

It isn't really a restaurant, just a watering hole, but a stop at this famous bar is a Bimini must. It was a favorite of writer Ernest Hemingway. Don't miss the museum here, which has a collection of paintings and pictures recalling the bar's most famous patron.

END OF THE WORLD BAR, $
Alice Town, no telephone
Dress code: casual
Reservations: not required

This supercasual bar had its 15 minutes of fame when the late Congressman Adam Clayton Powell used to hang out here. He was something of a local hero. The angler is remembered with an annual fishing tournament. Drop by for a rum punch at the sand floor bar and bring along something to add to the collection of clothing, business cards, caps, and more that fill every available inch of wall space.

GULFSTREAM BAR, $
Bimini Big Game Fishing Club And Hotel
Alice Town, ☎ 242/347-3391
www.bimini-big-game-club.com
Dress code: casual
Reservations: not required

This bar opens after the Barefoot Bar closes and stays open late. A favorite stop for the often praised rum punch and a nice place to hang out and enjoy a relaxed atmosphere.

GULFSTREAM RESTAURANT, $$-$$$
Bimini Big Game Fishing Club And Hotel
Alice Town, ☎ 242/347-3391
Dress code: casually elegant
Reservations: recommended

This breakfast and dinner restaurant serves seafood, chicken, steaks and more. It also offers an extensive wine list. A quiet, romantic choice.

Where To Stay

BIMINI BIG GAME
FISHING CLUB AND HOTEL, $$-$$$
Alice Town
☎ 800/737-1007, 242/347-3391, fax 347-3392
www.bimini-big-game-club.com

Probably the best known accommodation in the Biminis, this hotel offers 49 guest rooms and plenty of fishing opportunities as well as scuba diving. The hotel is also home to the Gulfstream Restaurant, Gulfstream Bar and the Barefoot Bar.

BIMINI BLUE WATER RESORT, $-$$
Alice Town
☎ 242/347-3066, fax 242/347-3293

This resort is located on a marina with full boating facilities. Guests can select from rooms with two double beds, suites with two bedrooms and a sitting room, and the three-bedroom cottage with kitchen. The resort is home to The Anchorage Restaurant.

COMPLEAT ANGLER HOTEL, $-$$
Alice Town
☎ 242/347-3122, fax 242/347-3293

☀ Hemingway buffs might enjoy a stay at this small hotel where the literary giant once stayed. The public areas display photos of the writer. The 12-room hotel is now part of the Blue Water Resort (above).

Between Meals

The Compleat Angler Hotel
Alice Town
Drop by for a look at the Hemingway memorabilia and even some of his writings.

Fountain of Youth
South Bimini
Hire a local guide or rent a car to find this pool near the airport (there is a marker). This site is allegedly the Fountain of Youth that Ponce De Leon was in search of in 1513.

People-to-People
☎ 242/326-5371, 242/328-7810
The People-to-People program is an excellent way to learn more about Bahamian residents and culture. This program matches vacationers with more than 1,500 Bahamian volunteers for a day of activities that might include shopping at a local market, dinner with a local family, fishing, boating, or a tour of back street sights.

Working Off Those Meals

☯ Scuba Diving

The mysterious **Bimini Wall**, a site that some say was either a road or part of the Lost City of Atlantis, is a favorite scuba destination. Scuba diving is available from **Bimini Undersea Adventures**, ☎ 242/347-3089.

☯ Sport Fishing

Numerous operators will take serious anglers out for a half- or full-day of big game fishing for bluefin tuna, tarpon, dolphin, amberjack, white and blue marlin, swordfish, barracuda, grouper and shark. Several marinas in Alice Town have fishing boats for charter, as well as guides. Check at the marina offices or ask at your hotel. The Bahamas Out Islands Promotion Board can provide more information. Call them at ☎ 800/688-4752 or 242/352-8044.

Cat Island

Cat Island is home of the highest peak in the Bahamas: all 206 feet of it. **Mount Alvernia** isn't exactly the stuff of nosebleeds, but it does lend an interesting summit to this large island, the sixth largest in the Bahamas. Cat Island is 325 miles southeast of Miami (and not at all the same piece of land as private Cat Cay, located in the Biminis).

Two theories account for the name of this island: wild cats that supposedly were descended from ones left by Spanish colonists and Captain Arthur Catt, a British sea captain (and sometimes termed a pirate).

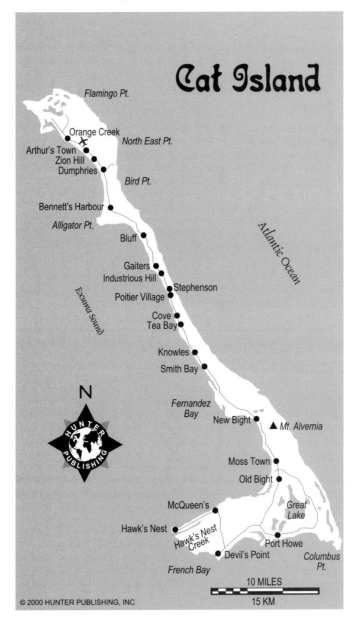

Recommended Restaurants

GREENWOOD BEACH RESORT, $$
☎ *242/342-3053*
Dress code: casual
Reservations: suggested

Dine outdoors at the beachside restaurant that serves Bahamian and international cuisine. The roofed terrace is one of the best spots for lunch, offering a casual atmosphere and a break from the sun. For dinner, head indoors to the dining room, also casual and decorated in island colors.

HAWK'S NEST RESORT, $$
☎ *242/357-7257*
Dress code: casually elegant
Reservations: required

Located near the marina, this restaurant serves up Bahamian cuisine as well as American dishes. Open for breakfast, lunch, and dinner. The restaurant has a warm, cozy feel with both wooden and stone walls scattered around to separate the intimate tables.

Where To Stay

GREENWOOD BEACH RESORT, $
Cat Island Dive Centre, Port Howe
☎ *800/688-4752, 242/342-3053 (phone and fax)*
www.greenwoodbeachresort.com

A favorite with divers, this 20-room resort is located on eight miles of beach. All rooms have private baths. The resort includes an excellent restaurant (see above).

HAWK'S NEST RESORT AND MARINA, $$$
Hawk's Nest
☎ *800/OUT-ISLAND, 242/357-7257 (phone and fax)*
www.hawks-nest.com

Ten guest rooms offer quiet privacy at this hotel, which has its own airstrip. Rooms feature air-conditioning, ceiling fans, and private baths; guests have access to a clubhouse, restaurant, and beach.

Between Meals

Columbus Point
Locals believe this Arawak cave is where Christopher Columbus first made landfall in the New World. It's located on the southeast point of the island.

The Hermitage at Mt. Alvernia
New Bight
A replica of a European hermitage, this meditation spot was built by Father Jerome in the 1940s using limestone from Mt. Alvernia. Situated just to the east of the town of New Bight.

Crooked Island & Acklins Island

Crooked and Acklins Islands almost look like one landmass, but are separated by the Crooked Island Passage. These islands were once the home of Loyalists who left America after the Revolution and came to settle on these islands surrounded by shallow water.

The Bahamas

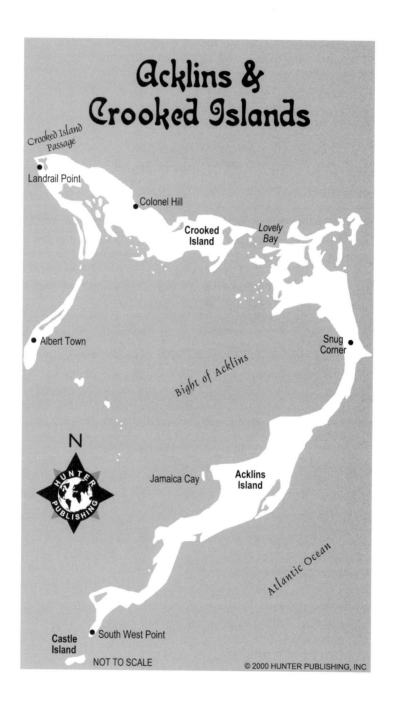

Acklins & Crooked Islands

Crooked Island Passage

Landrail Point

Colonel Hill

Crooked Island

Lovely Bay

Albert Town

Snug Corner

Bight of Acklins

N

HUNTER PUBLISHING

Jamaica Cay

Acklins Island

Atlantic Ocean

Castle Island

South West Point

NOT TO SCALE

© 2000 HUNTER PUBLISHING, INC

Crooked Island was called "Isabella" by Columbus in honor of his queen. Today it's a quiet place where visitors find many beautiful beaches. Located 240 miles from Nassau, this crooked piece of land is home to only 700 residents.

Acklins Island is separated from Crooked Island by a one-mile stretch of water. If you've got a bad case of the "been there, done that," Acklins may be a good destination for you. Few people visit here, but those who do find scuba diving, fishing, and swimming.

Where To Stay

The one accommodation on these charming islands is small and simple.

PITTSTOWN POINT LANDING, $
Landrail Point
☎ *242/344-2507, 800/PLACE-ZB, fax 242/344-2507*
www.pittstown.com

This 12-room resort is on Crooked Island's northwestern shore. Popular with private pilots because of its landing strip, the resort is also accessible on scheduled BahamasAir flights. Rooms here hug the beach. Activities include scuba diving (there is a great reef just offshore), bonefishing, deep-sea fishing, shuffleboard and volleyball.

The hotel recently completed Ozzie's Café, a dining room that serves breakfast, lunch and dinner. Guests sign up at breakfast for the dinner entrée of their choice that evening.

Eleuthera & Harbour Island

Eleuthera is an easy island to remember during those times when you're stuck in the office and fantasizing about an island getaway. In Greek, Eleuthera means "Freedom" and today it's a favorite retreat for those looking for a few days of freedom from hectic schedules.

To the first English settlers, that freedom meant religious freedom. The Eleutheran adventurers came to this land because it resembled English farmland. Located 60 miles east of Nassau, Eleuthera is hilly and fertile, and today it is the most developed of any of the Bahamian Out Islands.

Ask a local resident about his island, however, and he'll call it Cigatoo, the local name for this 200-square-mile piece of property. Whatever you call it, you'll find plenty of fun, including numerous dive sites, snorkeling, bonefishing, and more.

Just two miles off Eleuthera's northern coast lies **Harbour Island,** connected to its larger cousin by ferry service. This three-mile-long island is just half a mile wide, but it is the home of several attractions. Much of the activity takes place in **Dunmore Town**, where the streets are lined with clapboard houses, most with beautiful gardens. And just what do locals call Harbour Island? Briland. Local residents are known as Brilanders.

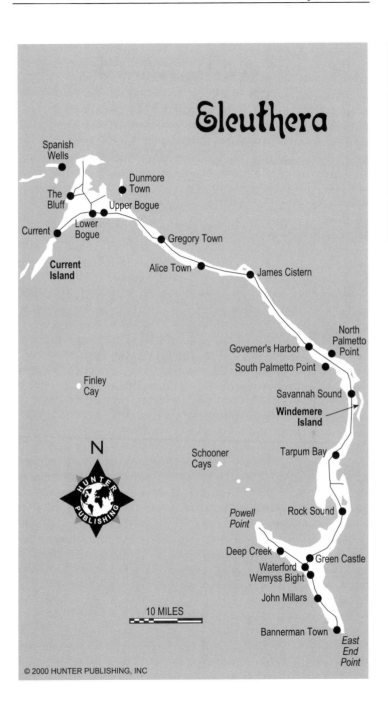

Eleuthera

Spanish Wells

Dunmore Town

The Bluff

Upper Bogue

Lower Bogue

Current

Current Island

Gregory Town

Alice Town

James Cistern

North Palmetto Point

Governer's Harbor

South Palmetto Point

Finley Cay

Savannah Sound

Windemere Island

N

Schooner Cays

Tarpum Bay

HUNTER PUBLISHING

Powell Point

Rock Sound

Deep Creek

Green Castle

Waterford

Wemyss Bight

John Millars

10 MILES

Bannerman Town

East End Point

© 2000 HUNTER PUBLISHING, INC

Recommended Restaurants

THE BLUE BAR, $$
Pink Sands Resort, Harbour Island
☎ 242/333-2030
Dress code: casual
Reservations: not required

This beach bar brings typical lunchtime fare up several notches with dishes such as Bahamian conch chowder spiked with dark rum, conch and cilantro fritters with Pickapeppa mayo, and West Indian chicken spring rolls with tandoori pineapple dip. The atmosphere is casual and many folks come here for lunch before an afternoon on the beach.

Cracked Tempura Cajun Conch with Salsa, Pink Sands Resort

Conch:

- *8 fresh conch*
- *1 teaspoon Cajun spice*
- *1 tablespoon virgin olive oil*

Peel and clean conch. Split in half without cutting through completely. Place in a plastic bag and pound with a mallet until about ⅔ inch thick. Marinate in oil and Cajun spice for one hour.

Tempura Batter:

- *1 whole egg*
- *1⅓ cups iced water*
- *1 cup all-purpose flour*
- *2 teaspoons Cajun spice*

Whisk egg and iced water in a bowl then add flour and Cajun spice and 5-6 ice cubes. Test tempura. Good tempura rises quickly to the surface of the oil.

Dip conch in batter and deep fry at 170° C for 1-2 minutes until light brown. Drain on absorbent paper.

Salsa Fresca:

- *4 large, very ripe red plum tomatoes*
- *1 red onion*
- *1 garlic clove, peeled, smashed, and finely chopped*
- *1 small bunch fresh cilantro*
- *juice of one lime*
- *⅓ cup virgin olive oil*
- *salt and pepper to taste*

Put tomatoes into a bowl and cover with boiling water. Leave for 10 seconds. Refresh in cold water and peel. Dice finely and put in a bowl. Peel and dice onion to same size and add. Finely chop cilantro and garlic and stir in with tomato. Pour over lime juice and olive oil. Season and leave for one hour. Serve along with conch and lime wedges. *Serves four.* ☀

■ ■

PINK SANDS MAIN DINING ROOM, $$$
Pink Sands, Harbour Island
☎ 242/333-2030
Dress code: Casually elegant
Reservations: recommended

Breakfast and dinner are served at this al fresco eatery. Filled with teak furniture that echoes the tropical surroundings, the intimate main dining room affords candlelit tables and a romantic atmosphere. Dinner always features a pre-set menu with a four-course meal, including appetizer, soup or salad, entrée, dessert, and coffee or tea. Favorite appetizers include tuna and sweet potato cakes with cilantro and soya dressing; Thai shrimp sautéed in sesame seed oil and lemon grass; and Bahamian sushi roll with mango, cucumber and conch. Dinner entrées include choices such as blackened grouper; cornmeal dusted Cornish game hen served on spinach and a tamarind-honey vinaigrette; or local fresh lobster tail with cilantro and sesame butter. Dinner is served from 7pm to 9pm; room service is also available.

Thai Wrapped Shrimp, Pink Sands

- *1 tablespoon black and white sesame seeds*
- *16 to 20 black tiger shrimp*
- *1 teaspoon Ga-Pi (shrimp paste)*
- *1 tablespoon sweet soya sauce*
- *9 super-thin spring roll skins*
- *1 tablespoon sesame oil*
- *2 ounces cilantro*
- *1 tablespoon sake*
- *1 ounce fresh ginger*
- *1 stalk lemon grass*
- *1 ounce garlic*
- *cracked black pepper and salt to taste*
- *1 egg*

Peel and clean the shrimp. In a food blender, finely chop the garlic, cilantro, ginger, lemon grass, Ga-Pi, soya, sake, sesame oil, salt, and pepper.

Add the shrimp to this mixture and marinate for at least six hours in the refrigerator. Cut egg roll wraps in half. Beat the egg and season.

Place a shrimp at one end of the egg roll and fold slowly, making sure the ends are tightly covered. Dip each one into the egg wash and sprinkle with sesame seeds. Deep fry at 325° for about three to four minutes and serve. *Serves four.*

Chef's Tip: "I find a good sweet and sour plum sauce or a light teriyaki dip complements this dish." ☀

Where To Stay

CLUB MED ELEUTHERA, $$
Governor's Harbour
☎ *800/CLUB MED, 242/332-2270, fax 242/332-2855*

This all-inclusive is a favorite with families due to their special kids' programs for children two years and older. Petit, Mini, and Kids Clubs offer plenty of activity for young vacationers, and adults find lots of action as well: bocce ball, circus workshops, golf, fishing, sailing, scuba diving, soccer, softball, tennis. Three restaurants offer plenty of dining options.

Note: This excellent resort was damaged by Hurricane Floyd in September, 1999. The property has closed temporarily and expects to reopen July 1st, 2000.

CORAL SANDS HOTEL
Dunmore Town, Harbour Island
☎ *242/333-2350, fax 242/333-2368*

This 23-room resort is reached by taxi and ferry. Some rooms have private balconies with a beach view, kitchens, and refrigerators. Guest amenities include fishing, sailing, snorkeling, swimming, tennis, and a dining room.

Grouper Coral Sands, Coral Sands Hotel

- *1½ pounds grouper filet, cut into bite-size pieces*
- *¼ pound butter*
- *1 cup lime juice*
- *1 tablespoon salt*
- *2½ cloves garlic, sliced*
- *1 onion, sliced*
- *1 quart sour cream*
- *¼ cup dried parsley*

Marinate grouper in a large bowl with sliced onions, lime juice, and salt. Allow to sit for 5 minutes. Drain grouper and sauté in frying pan with butter, sliced garlic and dried parsley (5 mins.). Add sour cream last. May be served in small bowls with toast points. *Serves six.* ☀

■ ■

PINK SANDS, $$$-$$$$
Harbour Island
☎ *800/OUTPOST, 242/333-2030, fax 242/333-2060*
www.islandoutpost.com

This resort offers 21 one-bedroom cottages and four two-bedroom cottages with a living room area. Located on, yes, a pink sand beach, the resort boasts a laid-back atmosphere. Guests enjoy a freshwater pool, three tennis courts (one lit for night play), exercise studio, Club House, library, and more. The resort can arrange for golf cart and bicycle rentals as well.

Two restaurants serve local dishes with a gourmet flair. The Blue Bar serves lunch right on the beach, while breakfast and dinner are offered in the main dining area.

Roast Lobster Tail & Oriental Hollandaise, Pink Sands

- *4 sweet Bahamian lobster tails (crawfish)*
- *2 ounces shiitake mushrooms*
- *1 tablespoon rice wine vinegar*
- *2 scallions*
- *1 ounce pickled ginger*
- *1 teaspoon chili paste*
- *1 clove of garlic*
- *1 tablespoon sweet oyster sauce*
- *8 ounces butter*
- *4 egg yolks*
- *½ ounce parsley*
- *½ sweet red pepper*
- *1 ounce sweet shallots*
- *½ ounce cilantro*
- *½ ounce sweet basil*
- *½ cup peanut oil*
- *lime juice*
- *salt and pepper to taste*

Lobster:

Prepare the lobster by cutting down the back with a heavy knife and pulling the meat out to rest on the shell. Season and place on a tray with a little water (this helps create steam to moisten the lobster when cooking). Bake in oven at 350° F for 10 to 15 minutes.

Hollandaise Sauce:

Finely chop the ginger, garlic, shallots, shiitake mushrooms, cilantro, red pepper, scallions, parsley, and sweet basil. Sauté these ingredients in peanut oil until tender and set aside. Boil the rice wine vinegar, transfer it to a bowl, and let it cool. Add egg yolks. Place the bowl over a pan of hot water and whisk to a sabayon. (A sabayon is created by cooking and thickening the egg yolks. When the yolks have been whisked to a thick consistency, remove from heat and slowly incorporate the warm clarified butter.) Add the already cooked ingredients with salt, pepper, oyster sauce, and a squeeze of lime juice. Cover hot lobster with sauce.

Chef's Tip: The chef recommends coconut rice and stir-fried vegetables with this dish. ☀

■ ■

RAMORA BAY CLUB, $$
Harbour Island
☎ 242/333-2325, fax 242/333-2500

This 38-room hotel is located on a hillside with a harbor view. Most rooms have a patio or balcony; some offer kitchens. Recreational options include scuba, windsurfing, sailing, tennis, and a beach. A dining room – serving breakfast, lunch, and dinner – is located on property.

Between Meals

People-to-People
☎ 242/326-5371, 242/328-7810, 242/356-0435-8,
fax 242/356-0434
The People-to-People program is an excellent way to learn more about Bahamian residents and culture. This program matches vacationers with more than 1,500 Bahamian volunteers for a day of activities that might include shopping at a local market, dinner with a local family, fishing, boating, or a tour of back street sights.

The Exuma Islands

The Exumas are a whole chain of islands and cays – over 350 of them, to be precise. Located right in the middle of the Islands of the Bahamas, the Exumas are a favorite destination for the sailing crowd.

Great & Little Exuma

© 2000 HUNTER PUBLISHING, INC

Most of the activity takes place on Great Exuma in the community of **George Town**, where shoppers visit the Straw Market. A far cry from the two-story version in Nassau, this local outdoor market is very relaxed. There's also good deep-sea fishing and diving in these islands. Staniel Cay's **Thunderball Grotto** was used in the filming of the James Bond movie *Thunderball*. At **Highborne Cay Wreck**, snorkelers can see a wreck in just 40 feet of water.

Recommended Restaurants

CLUB PEACE AND PLENTY, $$
☎ *242/336-2551*
Dress code: casual
Reservations: optional

This eatery serves breakfast, lunch and dinner and specializes in Bahamian as well as American cuisine. Start with a drink at the indoor bar or at the Reef Bar on the pool deck.

Conch Burgers, Club Peace and Plenty

- *2 tablespoons tomato paste*
- *2 pounds conch meat, chopped*
- *½ stalk celery, diced finely*
- *½ small onion, diced finely*
- *¾ cup cracker meal*
- *1 cup breadcrumbs*
- *salt and hot pepper to taste*

Combine all ingredients in a large bowl and mix well. Season with salt and hot pepper. Create round patties from mixture. Heat oil in frying pan and place patties in pan, cooking for three minutes or until lightly brown. Serve on bun with lettuce and tomato. *Serves five.* ⚬

HOTEL HIGGINS LANDING, $$-$$$
Stocking Island, ☎ 800/688-4752, 242/336-2460
www.higginslanding.com
Dress code: casually elegant
Reservations: required

A gourmet menu featuring local seafood with a chef's special touches brings guests to this hotel restaurant. Dining is available indoors by candlelight or outdoors.

STANIEL CAY YACHT CLUB, $$
Staniel Cay, ☎ 242/355-2011
Dress code: casual, casually elegant
Reservations: optional

Yachties can pick up a boxed lunch or enjoy breakfast, lunch, or dinner at this fun-loving club. A great place to visit with fellow travelers and share stories, especially salty tales.

Where To Stay

CLUB PEACE AND PLENTY, $$
George Town
☎ *800/525-2210, 242/336-2551, fax 242/336-2093*
E-mail: pandp@peaceandplenty.com

This 35-room waterside hotel offers air-conditioned accommodations with harbor-view balconies. This inn has had an illustrious guest list, including HRH Prince Phillip and HRM King Constantine of Greece. Amenities include a freshwater pool, twice-weekly cocktail parties and plenty of beach fun – snorkeling, exploring undersea caves, sailing – at Stocking Island Beach Club. The club has a snack bar.

HOTEL HIGGINS LANDING, $$$
Stocking Island
☎ *800/688-4752, ☎/fax 242/336-2460*
www.higginslanding.com

This eco-friendly resort is home to five cottages, each furnished with antiques, queen-size bed, private bath and ceiling fan. The property, which took four years to construct, was designed to be harmonious with its natural surroundings. Guests can select from swimming off Silver Palms Beach or exploring Turtle Lagoon on the other side of the resort (an area also favored for bonefishing).

The hotel is the only property on Stocking Island. In 1997 it was awarded the EcoTourism Award from *Islands* magazine, who said it was the best eco-tourist resort in The Bahamas.

PEACE AND PLENTY BEACH INN, $$
George Town (see above for details)

This beachside hotel has 16 guest rooms, each with air-conditioning, ceiling fan and private balconies. Shuttle bus service into George Town is available.

PEACE AND PLENTY BONEFISH LODGE, $$
George Town (see above for details)

Bonefishermen, not surprisingly, make up much of the guest list at this eight-room property. Facilities include a fisherman's lounge, game room, fly-tying facitlities, tackle and pro shop, satellite television, video library and a sport art gallery.

STANIEL CAY YACHT CLUB, $$
Staniel Cay, ☎ 242/355-2024, fax 242/355-2044

This waterfront property offers cottages for two to four guests and a guest house for seven. Travelers have use of a marina, scuba diving equipment and Boston Whalers.

Between Meals

People-to-People
☎ 242/326-5371, 242/328-7810, fax 242/356-0434
For more information on this program, see pages 24-26.

Grand Bahama

Grand Bahama island is indeed a grand destination, starting with the city of **Freeport**. The **Port Lucaya Marketplace and Marina** has shops selling perfumes, clothing, and crafts, and usually has live music along the waterfront. You'll find goods from around the globe at the **International Bazaar**, and nearby the **Bahamas Arts and Crafts Market** sells locally made jewelry and baskets. The bazaar and market are adjacent to the **Resort at Bahamia**, where you can try your luck at table games or slots.

The city of Freeport/Lucaya was established just over 40 years ago as a tax-free base for trading nations of the west.

Blue Holes

The seabed around the Bahamas is dotted with deep, seemingly bottomless holes that are easily visible from the air. The geological oddities were formed when an underwater mountain range filled with glaciers during the Ice Age. As the glaciers grew, water levels dropped and the land peaked up from the sea. Once the glaciers melted, the sea floor became pocked with numerous holes and caverns. Many of these have never been explored, although some, such as Gold Rock Blue Hole, have interested divers and geologists for some time.

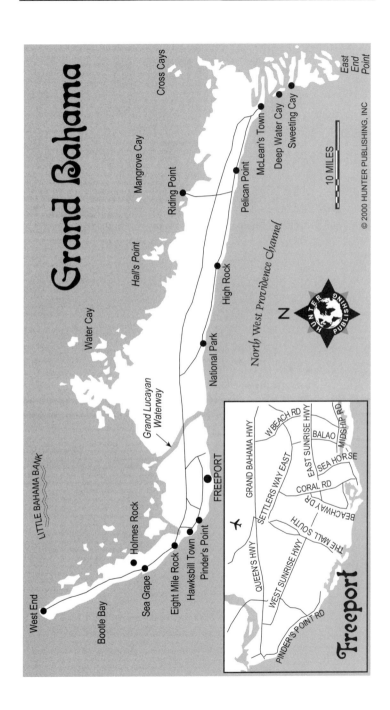

Grand Bahama

Recommended Restaurants

CROWN ROOM, $$$
Resort at Bahamia
Freeport, ☎ *242/352-9661*
Dress code: dressy, jacket required
Reservations: required

☀ This gourmet eatery serves continental cuisine in an elegant atmosphere that includes mirrors, crystal chandeliers and muted lighting.

GUANAHANI'S, $$-$$$
Resort at Bahamia
Freeport, ☎ *242/352-9661*
Dress code: casually elegant
Reservations: suggested

☀ Overlooking the pool, this Bahamian-style restaurant boasts a tropical atmosphere complete with rattan chairs, verdant palms, and ceiling fans. Bahamian specialties fill the menu. You'll find native grouper and barbecue spareribs.

MORGAN'S BLUFF RESTAURANT, $$-$$$
Resort at Bahamia
Freeport, ☎ *242/352-9661*
Dress code: casually elegant
Reservations: suggested

☀ This dinner-only restaurant serves up Bahamian specialties such as conch chowder, conch salad, cracked conch, conch fritters, and other seafood as well. Located in the Princess Tower, this restaurant has a delightful nautical theme.

Cracked Conch, Morgan's Bluff Restaurant

- *4 conch*
- *2 eggs*
- *½ cup milk*
- *flour (enough to coat conch)*

Beat conch until tender. Mix eggs and milk in a large bowl. Dip conch in flour until completely covered, then place in milk and egg batter. Drain conch for about two minutes then place in flour again. Fry in oil until lightly-medium browned. *Serves four.* ☀

■ ■

RIB ROOM, $$$
Resort at Bahamia
Freeport, ☎ *242/352-9661*
Dress code: casually elegant or dressy
Reservations: suggested

This formal steakhouse serves seafood and steaks, all in a masculine atmosphere that includes rough-hewn timber-beamed ceilings and red leather chairs.

Where To Stay

CLARION ATLANTIK BEACH, $$
Freeport, ☎ *242/373-1444, fax 242/373-7481*

This 175-room resort is located on Lucaya Beach and offers an array of watersports and beach fun plus parasailing. Some rooms include kitchens, microwaves, refrigerators, and more.

CLUB FORTUNA BEACH, $$
Freeport, ☎ *242/373-4000, fax 242/373-6181*

This all-inclusive resort has a Mediterranean feel and over 200 guest rooms. It offers a full range of activities, including sailing, windsurfing, snorkeling, tennis, a golf driving range and nightly entertainment. Scuba diving and waterskiing can be arranged for an additional fee.

PORT LUCAYA RESORT AND YACHT CLUB, $$
Bell Channel Road, ☎ *242/373-6618, fax 242/373-6652*

☀ This 160-room resort is adjacent to the Port Lucaya Marketplace. Guests have beach access as well as a playground, marina, restaurant and pool.

RESORT AT BAHAMIA, $$-$$$$
Freeport, ☎ *242/352-9661, fax 242/352-2542*

☀ Guest rooms at this sprawling resort (formerly the Bahamas Princess Resort & Casino) include 400 rooms in the 10-story tower as well as 565 two and three-story low-rise accommodations. All rooms have two double beds, cable TV, direct dial telephone, and a host of other comforts. The resort has a wide array of dining options, including Guanahani's, the Rib Room, Morgan's Bluff, and Crown Room (for more details on these establishments, see above).

Between Meals

Bahamas Arts and Crafts Market
Freeport
Hours: daily, sunrise to sunset
Admission: free
This market sells locally made jewelry and baskets. Located adjacent to the Resort at Bahamia.

Garden of the Groves Botanical Garden
Lucaya
Hours: afternoons; closed Mondays
Admission: fee
This 12-acre botanical garden is home to over 5,000 varieties of flowers, trees, and shrubs.

International Bazaar
Freeport
Hours: 10-6, Monday to Saturday
Admission: free

The atmosphere is global at this international bazaar. Here narrow streets feature many types of architecture and shops showcasing merchandise from distant lands. Cuisines from around the world yield an exotic touch to this shopping district.

Lucayan National Park
Grand Bahama Highway, ☎ *242/352-5738*
Hours: daily, sunrise to sunset
Admission: free
This 40-acre park is filled with mangroves, pine, and palm trees. There are also six miles of charted caves, a secluded beach, hiking trails, and picnic areas. This park is home to an enormous network of underwater caves, although diving is prohibited without a permit from ENEXSO (☎ 242/373-1244, fax 242/373-8956) and even swimming in the caves is a no-no.

People-to-People
☎ *242/352-8044, fax 242/352-2714*
For details on this unique program, see pages 24-26.

Port Lucaya Marketplace and Marina
Lucaya
Hours: 10-6, Monday to Saturday
Admission: free
Another favorite stop of ours is the Port Lucaya Marketplace and Marina. Here shops offer perfumes, clothing, and crafts. Live music along the outdoor waterfront usually keeps the atmosphere lively.

Rand Memorial Nature Centre
East Settler's Way, Freeport
☎ *242/352-5438*
Hours: 9-4, Monday through Friday, 1-4 on Saturday
Admission: fee
The Rand Memorial Nature Centre is home to over 200 species of birds. You'll also find a replica of a Lucayan village.

UNEXSO's The Dolphin Experience
☎ *800-992-DIVE*
Hours: daily
Admission: fee

Here you can experience a close-up encounter with these marine mammals. Be sure to call for a reservation; slots are limited.

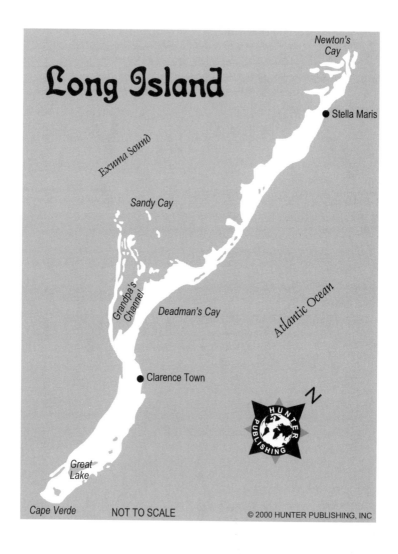

Long Island

It's not hard to guess how this island got its name. Stretching 60 miles end to end (although only four miles across) Long Island lives up to its moniker. This quiet getaway is a favorite with divers, anglers, and boaters. It offers quiet beaches, and a gentle, rolling landscape.

Like other Bahamian islands, this one was settled by many Loyalists who came here after the American Revolution. If you take a guided ride around the island, you'll see the ruins of several plantation homes that once led large cotton estates.

While on your tour, you might stop by several other Long Island attractions. **Dunmore's Cave** was once used by pirates. You can also see the Moorish-style **churches** built by Father Jerome. And don't miss **Cape Santa Maria** on the north end of the island, the site where Columbus first anchored and named this land Fernandina.

Recommended Restaurants

CAPE SANTA MARIA, $$-$$$
Stella Maris, ☎ *242/338-5273*
Dress code: casually elegant
Reservations: required

Dine on Bahamian specialties as well as American and continental fare at this seaside restaurant. Meals are accompanied by a fine selection of wines. Breakfast, lunch and dinner are served, but each at a preset time; call for times. Like the resort itself, the restaurant is charming and relaxed – the perfect place to unwind.

The Bahamas

STELLA MARIS RESORT CLUB DINING ROOM, $$
Stella Maris Resort Club, Stella Maris
☎ 242/338-2051
Dress code: casually elegant
Reservations: suggested

In this garden setting, diners enjoy Bahamian, American, and European cuisine. The restaurant offers many special events, such as barbecues and dinner cruises. The atmosphere here is homey and relaxed and – after just a few days on property – filled with familiar faces.

Where To Stay

CAPE SANTA MARIA BEACH RESORT AND FISHING CLUB, $$$-$$$$
Stella Maris
☎ 800/663-7090, 242/338-5273, fax 242/338-6013
E-mail: capesantamaria@batelnet.bs; www.obmg.com

These 12 accommodations include one- and two-bedroom villas on a four-mile beach. The beachfront cottages, all built in a colonial style, have air-conditioning. And there's plenty of activity – windsurfing, fishing, snorkeling, bicycling and more.

STELLA MARIS RESORT CLUB, $$-$$$
Stella Maris
☎ 800-426-0466, 242/338-2050, fax 242/338-2052
E-mail: smrc@stellamarisresort.com
www.stellamarisresort.com

This 50-room resort includes one-bedroom cottages and two- and four-bedroom villas. Each is air-conditioned and has ceiling fans and refrigerators. Guests can enjoy snorkeling, scuba diving, fishing, cruises and sailing.

New Providence Island

☀ Just a half-hour flight from Miami, this island may be just a stone's (or a conch shell's) throw from the US mainland, but Nassau gives visitors a wonderful taste of Caribbean life. The atmosphere is a delightful combination of British and Caribbean.

Both locals and vacationers tend to use the term "Nassau" to identify the island of New Providence, but the city proper is located on the north side of the island. It is a compact city filled with activity, especially along **Bay Street**, where locals and visitors shop for duty-free items. Just blocks away, the seat of the Bahamian government operates in buildings the color of a conch shell. Downtown Nassau offers several inexpensive hotels that utilize nearby public beaches.

Prince George Dock always bustles with cruise ship passengers enjoying the city for the day. From the cruise port you'll also see a tall, curving bridge that leads to **Paradise Island**. Nicknamed the "Monaco of the Bahamas," this is the most luxurious area of New Providence Island. Once named Hog Island, this area was revitalized by the investment of Donald Trump, Merv Griffin and South African businessman Sol Kerzner, who renovated the **Atlantis Hotel** at the cost of $1 million a day – every day – for a six-month building period. The island is also home of **The Cloisters**, the ruins of a 14th-century French monastery that were purchased by William Randolph Hearst in the 1920s and later moved to the island.

Tourists also flock to **Cable Beach**, 10 minutes west of downtown Nassau. This stretch of sand is lined with high-rise ho-

The Bahamas

tels and some of the island's hottest nightspots. Shuttles run between these resorts and Nassau several times daily.

Beyond these two resort areas, the island moves at a quieter pace. If you crave tranquillity, head to the south shore, about a 30-minute ride from downtown. Here, beneath willowy casuarina trees, couples can enjoy privacy and beautiful beaches that give way to a shallow sea.

Cacique Award

The chefs of The Bahamas are now being recognized for their culinary skills with the Cacique Award Hotel Chef of the Year. Cacique is a word that meant "chieftain" to the Lucayan Indians who first inhabited The Bahamas. Every year the Ministry of Tourism recognizes those who have made outstanding contributions to the hospitality industry with Cacique Awards and a special category recognizes the top hotel chefs.

The winner of the 1998 Cacique Hotel Chef of the Year went to **Charles Smith**, *Executive Chef at the Radisson Grand Resort. Finalists included Kerry Robinson, Sous Chef at Nassau Marriott Resort and Crystal Palace Casino and Tracey Sweeting, Sous Chef, Atlantis, Paradise Island.*

In 1997/1997, the award for Hotel Chef of the Year went to **Edwin Johnson**, *Executive Chef, Nassau Marriott Resort and Crystal Palace Casino. Finalists that year included Pedro Bain, Head Chef, Cafe Martinique, Atlantis, Paradise Island and Charles Smith, Executive Chef, Radisson Grand Resort.*

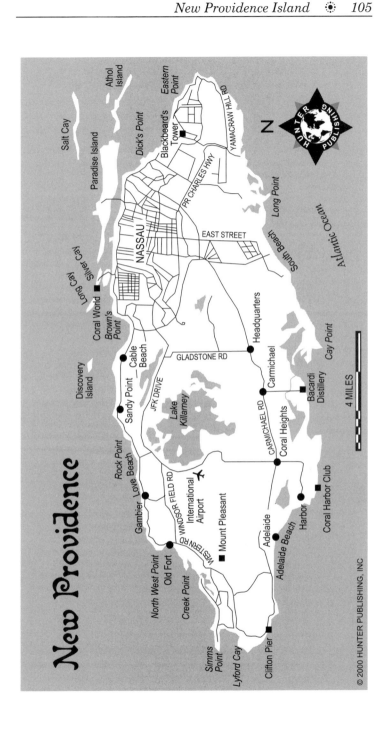

Recommended Restaurants

THE AMICI RESTAURANT, $$-$$$
Radisson Cable Beach, ☎ *242/327-6000*
Dress code: casually elegant
Reservations: suggested

Traditional Italian cuisine is the specialty of the house at this romantic two-story garden dining room. Two wooden gazebos, mahogany columns, marble floors, and a handpainted ceiling create a special ambience. The restaurant also boasts an extensive wine list.

ANDROSIA STEAK AND SEAFOOD RESTAURANT, $$$
Cable Beach Shoppers Haven, ☎ *242/327-7805*
Dress code: casually elegant
Reservations: suggested

The specialty of this dinner-only restaurant is peppersteak au Paris. It's prepared using an heirloom recipe from Les Halles in Paris, a combination of Dijon mustard, cracked peppercorns, brandy and light cream. Other favorites here include Bahamian grouper, red snapper, lobster thermidor, fillet of flounder, shrimp, veal, and more.

ANTHONY'S CARIBBEAN GRILL, $-$$
East Casino Drive, Paradise Island
☎ *242/363-3152*
Dress code: casual
Reservations: optional

Located in the Paradise Village Shopping Centre, this fun-loving restaurant serves Bahamian and American dishes as well as some Jamaican favorites, such as pasta rasta. Families are enticed by a special kids menu; indoor and outdoor dining is available. A member of A Real Taste of the Bahamas program (see pages 24-26).

ATLAS BAR AND GRILL, $-$$
Atlantis, Paradise Island
☎ 242/636-3000
Dress code: casual
Reservations: not required

Part of the new Royal Towers at Atlantis, this bar and grill features a range of appetizers and entrées that are more than the usual snack fare. Along with the full menu, the restaurant has daily specials, which might be double grilled pork chop with caramelized apple or shrimp scampi with garlic, tomato and buttered noodles.

This elegant eatery, just steps from the casino floor, is a fun place to start your evening at Atlantis. The restaurant is casual and family-friendly, with a video bar and views of the new marina.

Atlantis, Paradise Island.

Sample Menu, Atlas Bar And Grill

☀ APPETIZERS: Smoked salmon omelette with bagel chips; roasted garlic soup with pumpkin and cranberry toast; San Daniele proscuitto, bushel of nachos; sweet corn and leek chowder with Bahamian lobster; Caesar salad.

☀ SANDWICHES: Smoked turkey with herbed apple-mustard spread, lentil sprouts; rare roast beef with balsamic onions, romaine lettuce, pepper aioli, kaiser roll; warm pastrami with red cabbage slaw, white cheddar, scallion on rye; classic BLT with hickory smoked bacon on toasted pullman loaf.

☀ PASTA AND PIZZA: Maltagliati Bolognese with fresh-cut pasta; mixed meat ragu; shaved ricotta salata; penne with broccoli; oven gridder (upside-down Chicago-style thick crust pizza).

☀ SIMPLY GRILLED: 8-ounce tenderloin of beef; 8-ounce tuna steak; 16-ounce T-bone steak; 14-ounce sirloin steak. All steaks are served with baked beans, corn on the cob, and a green salad.

☀ ENTREES: Roast chicken with artichoke, mushroom, fingerling potato gratin; the Atlas beefburger with ground Angus beef, tomato jam; smoked and slow-roasted baby back ribs with fennel slaw; whole deep-fried catfish; meat loaf of certified Angus beef .

☀ DESSERTS: Warm apple pie with English cream or à la mode; The Black Cow (carbonated root beer and vanilla ice cream); peanut parfait with roasted peanuts, bourbon ice cream, fudge brownies and praline sauce; Atlas cheesecake with fresh fruit compote; milk shake; s'mores.

☀ SNACK MENU: Potato skins with bacon, chives and sour cream; battered mushrooms with Southern Creole dip; spicy buffalo wings; corn dogs on a stick; chicken quesadilla; sweet potato fries; fish nibbles; giant pretzel and a beer.

AVERY'S RESTAURANT, $-$$
Adelaide Village off Carmichael Road
☎ 242/362-1547
Dress code: casually elegant
Reservations: optional

This restaurant serves Bahamian cuisine from souse to peas and rice. Additionally, it is well known for its conch fritters, made fresh. Located on South West Bay, Avery's offers diners free transportation from the southwest side of the island. A member of A Real Taste of the Bahamas program (see pages 24-26).

AVOCADO'S, $$$$
Radisson Cable Beach, ☎ 242/327-6000
Dress code: dressy
Reservations: required

This fine dining restaurant features an elegant decor, candlelit tables, and a romantic atmosphere – perfect for sharing with someone special. California, "Floribbean," and Bahamian influences are seen on its eclectic menu.

BACCARAT, all-inclusive
Sandals Royal Bahamian Resort And Spa
Cable Beach, ☎242/327-6400
Dress code: casually elegant
Reservations: required

Classic French gourmet dishes are the featured menu items here. Food is served to diners seated at tables overlooking the pool. The setting is as elegant as the meal itself, with tall, soaring windows that take in the beauty of this beachside resort. This is a good choice for a romantic evening out.

Sample Dinner Menu, Baccarat

☀ HORS D'OEUVRES: Mille Feuille Printanier (grilled fresh portobello mushrooms, sautéed buttered spinach, roast pumpkin napoleon served with cream of sun-dried tomatoes); Ravioli de Langoustine (homemade baby lobster ravioli with a herb-porcini mushroom sauce and baby scallops in a garlic butter); Assiette Gourmande (an array of smoked salmon, smoked poultry and Parma ham served with an artichoke and tomato sauce).

☀ SOUPS: Soupe de Tomate et Fromage (oven-smoked tomato, roasted leek and garlic Monterey jack soup); Soupe de Fenouil et Fruits de Mer (fennel roots, salted cod and shellfish chowder).

☀ SALADS: Assorted lettuce leaves, radiccio and endive served with gorgonzola, croutons, walnuts, pine nuts and olive oil vinaigrette.

☀ SUGGESTIONS DU CHEF: Magret de Canard (grilled honey breast of duck in a port wine sauce); Côte de Veau au Poivre (pan-seared veal chops with a three-peppercorn sauce); Canelonnide Poulet (tube pasta stuffed with smoked chicken, ricotta cheese and fresh herbs); St. Jacques en Croute (sautéed sea scallops laced in a chablis cream sauce with shiitake mushrooms baked in puff pastry); Panache de Poissons (assorted grilled fish fillet).

☀ DESSERTS: Chocolat et Mousse à la Menthe (layers of chocolate and mint mousse with a rich chocolate cake and fresh chocolate mint sauce); sherbet with a crisp cookie and tropical fruit sauces; Meringue Almond (almond-flavored meringue with wedges of oranges on a Grand Marnier and white chocolate sauce); Cappuccino Glace Torta (creamy coffee ice cream between thin nutty biscuits served with a rich chocolate sauce).

BAHAMIAN CLUB, $$$
Atlantis, Paradise Island, ☎ *242/636-3000*
Dress code: dressy
Reservations: required

This elegant eatery is filled with dark woods and white tablecloths. It serves up steaks and seafood nightly. Prime rib is a specialty.

Coconut Floating Island with Guava Brandy Sauce, Atlantis, Paradise Island

- *6 egg whites*
- *½ teaspoon salt*
- *2 ounces guava purée*
- *4 ounces sugar*
- *4 egg yolks*
- *1 teaspoon vanilla*
- *1 ounce brandy*
- *4 ounces whipping cream*
- *6 ounces milk*
- *4 ounces finely diced guava meat*
- *¼ bunch fresh mint*
- *toasted coconut shavings*

Add ½ teaspoon salt to a pot of water ⅔ full and bring to simmer. In mixing bowl, whip egg whites and 1 ounce of sugar to medium peak. With a serving spoon, place egg white mixture into simmering saltwater, one teaspoon at a time, poaching gently on both sides. Removed poached egg white and roll in toasted coconut.

In pot, over medium heat, cook guava purée with remaining sugar until sugar dissolves. Ignite mixture with brandy and remove from heat, allowing to cool. Add purée mixture, egg yolks, and vanilla to bowl and mix well. In saucepan, heat cream and milk, allowing it to scald. Removed from heat and add ½ cup to egg mixture to temper. Add tempered mixture to remaining milk and stir continuously with wooden spoon under low flame until sauce coats back of spoon. Strain sauce and add guava meat. Coat poached eggs in sauce. *Serves four.*

BAHAMIAN KITCHEN, $-$$
Trinity Place off Market or Bay Streets
☎ 242/325-0702
Dress code: casually elegant
Reservations: optional

Bahamian cuisine is the order of the day with dishes like pan-fried turtle steak prepared with sherry and onions, okra soup and white rice, and Bahamian seafood. A member of A Real Taste of the Bahamas Program (see pages 24-26).

BLACK ANGUS GRILLE, $$$
Nassau Marriott Resort and Crystal Palace Casino
Cable Beach, ☎ 242/327-6200, Ext. 6861
Dress code: dressy, jackets required
Reservations: required

This dinner-only restaurant serves steaks and seafood in an elegant atmosphere.

BUENA VISTA, $$-$$$
Delancy Street, ☎ 242/322-2811
Dress code: dressy, jacket suggested
Reservations: suggested

Both continental dishes and Bahamian cuisine are featured in this restaurant, a good choice for a special evening out. Menu offerings include specialties such as Bahamian lobster, red snapper with honey-mustard dressing, and rack of spring lamb Provençale. An extensive wine list complements the food.

The restaurant is housed in a historic 19th-century mansion and has been serving vacationers and residents since 1946. A member of A Real Taste of Bahamas program

CAFE GOOMBAY, all-inclusive
Sandals Royal Bahamian Resort and Spa
Cable Beach, ☎ 242/327-6400
Dress code: casually elegant
Reservations: required

This traditional Bahamian restaurant is located on the offshore island of Balmoral and is decorated in the brilliant colors of Junkanoo. A meal at this open-air eatery is a fun experience, with many dishes reflecting the local taste.

Sample Dinner Menu, Café Goombay

☀ APPETIZERS: Abaco Crab Cake (with avocado, pineapple, bell peppers, and olive oil salsa); Goombay Roll (stuffed with tender strips of conch and served with soya wasabi and mango sauces); Conch Paccio (assorted greens served with traditional conch salad; conch fritters; Smuddered Grouper (marinated grouper).

☀ SOUPS: Spanish Wells conch chowder (with diced vegetables, tomatoes, Scotch bonnet, pepper and a touch of Armagnac); Exuma Gumbo (with veggies, smoked bacon and baby dumplings).

☀ SALAD: Junkanoo Salad (assorted greens with your choice of exotic dressing).

☀ ENTREES: Conchy Delight (cracked conch, golden-fried, served with fresh herbs and tartar sauce); steamed morsels of tenderized conch coated with light smoked barbecue tomato coulis; Caribbean kebabs (with chicken, pineapple, beef, onions, and mushrooms); linguine pasta sautéed with conch and a fresh tomato sauce; pan-seared red snapper crusted with honey, peanut and sesame seeds; charbroiled jerked lamb chops; steamed Caribbean shellfish and vegetables simmered bouillabaisse style; stir-fried gingered calamari and black tiger shrimp; minced crawfish (shredded local lobster) sautéed with vegetables, scallions and basil, laced with cilantro and tomato sauce.

☀ DESSERT: Guava Duff (a Bahamian dessert tradition consisting of guava-filled pastry, served with a warm sweet guava sauce); coconut tart (filled with shredded coconut cooked with ginger, cinnamon and rose water then baked and served with tropical fruit sauce); chocolate bread pudding served with a rum cream and chocolate sauce; pineapple and mango strudel with a tropical fruit sauce; orange chiffon cheesecake.

CAFE JOHNNY CANOE, $-$$
West Bay Street on Cable Beach
☎ *242/327-3373*
Dress code: casually elegant
Reservations: required

This is one of our favorite Bahamian restaurants, both for its festive atmosphere and its excellent food and service. Don't look for anything fancy; this is a diner-style restaurant decorated with Bahamian crafts and photos of the restaurant's long history. Diners can select from seating indoors and outside, a good choice on warm evenings, when you can share a drink beneath the multi-colored Christmas lights and listen to live music.

Breakfast, lunch, and dinner are served in this popular eatery. We opted for an appetizer of conch fritters followed by grouper entrées. Prime rib, Bahamian fried chicken, fried shrimp, cracked conch, and burgers round out the extensive menu. Follow it all with a Bahamian guava duff with light rum sauce. A member of A Real Taste of the Bahamas program.

CAFE MATISSE, $$-$$$
Bank Lane, behind Parliament Square
☎ *242/356-7012*
Dress code: proper attire required for dinner
Reservations: suggested

This downtown restaurant serves up Italian dishes – homemade pasta, seafood, and pizza. Open for lunch and dinner. Housed in a century-old building, the restaurant is filled with Matisse prints.

CAFFE DEL OPERA, $$-$$$
Bay Street, ☎ *242/356-6118*
Dress code: casually elegant or dressy
Reservations: suggested

This historic building – built more than a century ago – was once a church. Today the gospel music has been replaced by Italian opera, a perfect accompaniment to the regional Italian dishes that make this restaurant popular. Sicilian cuisine is the specialty of the house, served along

with a full seafood menu. Fresh, homemade pasta is always an option, or you can call ahead to order something special.

THE CAVE, $-$$
Atlantis, Paradise Island, ☎ *242/363-3000*
Dress code: casual
Reservations: not required

The fun thing about eating in this casual lunchtime burger diner is the setting: it is built as the authentic recreation of an actual Bahamian cave. Located just steps from the waterfalls and play area, this supercasual eatery is popular with families taking a quick break from the sun.

THE CELLAR, $$
11 Charlotte Street, ☎ *242/322-8877*
Dress code: casual
Reservations: optional

Bahamian and continental dishes are served at this restaurant, which served as a home at the turn of the century. Quiche, salads, pasta and sandwiches make light lunches, served Monday through Saturday in the restaurant and garden patio.

COLUMBUS TAVERN, $$-$$$
Paradise Island Drive, Paradise Island
☎ *242/363-2543*
Dress code: casually elegant
Reservations: recommended

This harborside restaurant offers an excellent view of the yachts coming and going. Offerings at this nautically themed eatery include lobster flambé, steak Diane, and many seafood delights.

COMFORT ZONE, $-$$
#5 Wulff Road
☎ *242/323-2676*
Dress code: casually elegant
Reservations: optional

American and Bahamian dishes bring in diners to this fun eatery. Choose from Bahamian favorites such as boiled fish, Bahamian-style potato salad, johnnycake, peas 'n rice, potato bread, souse, and more. A member of A Real Taste of the Bahamas program.

COMPASS POINT RESTAURANT, $$-$$$
Compass Point, West Bay Street, Gambier
☎ *242/327-4500*
Dress code: casually elegant
Reservations: suggested

☀ This oceanfront restaurant serves inventive cuisine using local ingredients. This open-air seaside eatery is as delightfully casual as the resort itself, the perfect place to throw on a colorful sundress and enjoy a Bahamian meal, all enjoyed to the sound of the surf. Chef Stephen Bastian's talents are showcased on a menu that features Californian-Caribbean cuisine. Breakfast, lunch and dinner are served here.

Compass Point.

Conch Chowder, Compass Point

- ¼ *cup canola oil*
- *4 conch, finely chopped*
- *3 bay leaves*
- *1 stalk fresh thyme*
- *1 teaspoon crushed black pepper*
- ¼ *Scotch bonnet pepper, finely chopped (can substitute any hot chile)*
- *1 large onion, coarsely chopped*
- *1 large carrot, coarsely chopped*
- *1 large potato, coarsely chopped*

- *1 red bell pepper, coarsely chopped*
- *1 rib celery, coarsely chopped*
- *8 cups fish stock or water*
- *1 ounce dark rum*
- *5 tablespoons butter*
- *5 tablespoons all-purpose flour*

Heat the oil, add the conch, thyme, black pepper, Scotch bonnet and bay leaves. Cook for five to seven minutes, stirring constantly. Add onion, carrot, potato, celery, and bell pepper and cook for five minutes. Add the rum and the stock or water. Bring to a boil and simmer for 10 minutes. Meanwhile, make a roux by melting butter over medium heat and whisking in flour; cook, whisking, until the roux is blond to brown in color and remove it from heat to cool down. Whisk roux into chowder and cook for half an hour over very low heat. Salt to taste. *Yield: four servings.* ☀

Chef Bastian's choices vary nightly, but you're likely to find some of these specialties.

Sample Dinner Menu, Compass Point

☀ Grilled and blackened fresh fish with local and Thai-influenced salsas and relishes.

☀ Conch chowder spiked with dark rum.

☀ Agnolotti filled with conch, sundried tomatoes and spinach and served with a tomato-basil cream sauce.

☀ Bahamian maki roll with conch, mango and cucumber served with wasabi and pickled ginger.

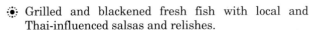

CONCH FRITTERS BAR AND GRILL, $
Marlborough Street
☎ *242/343-8778*
Dress code: casual
Reservations: not required

They claim to offer "the best conch fritters in town," so test for yourself. Both Bahamian and American dishes are served in a casual atmosphere. A member of A Real Taste of the Bahamas program.

THE CRYSTAL ROOM, all-inclusive
Sandals Royal Bahamian Resort And Spa
Cable Beach, ☎ *242 / 327-6400*
Dress code: casually elegant
Reservations: suggested

Elegant international fare is served à la carte at this restaurant which, like the resort itself, is for couples only.

Sample Dinner Menu, The Crystal Room

❖ APPETIZERS: Greek Tradition – grilled succulent slices of gyros, beef with tomato, onions and sweet pepper nestled in a pita pocket topped with tzatziki sauce; Chicken Teriyaki – tender pieces of chicken sauteed with bamboo shoots and pineapple laced in silky teriyaki sauce and served on a bed of wild rice; Seafood Carnival – a blend of shellfish laced with a cocktail sauce and fresh apple served on exotic fruits.

❖ SOUPS: West Indian Delicacy – conch slowly cooked with diced "ground provisions," a touch of cream and an abundance of local spices; Bahamian Dream – sweet potato, pumpkin and spiny lobster bisque.

❖ SALAD: A salad of Caribbean greens Caesar style, served with strips of cajun flying fish sautéed in garlic.

❖ ENTREES: Cajun Pork - marinated roast loin of pork with mustard, Cajun spices, served with a cracked peppercorn jus; Grilled leg of lamb with local spices served with fresh mint, and roasted onions; Vegetarian Cuisine – baby spinach, plum tomato, and three cheese lasagna gratinéed to perfection; Rigatoni alla carbonara – tube pasta cooked al dente served with a rich creamy sauce, roast pancetta and parmesan cheese sauce; Cioppino – Caribbean array of fish and shellfish, vegetables poached in a rich saffron fish stock; Sunset Delight – giant garden salad with sautéed garlic button mushrooms on French bread with mozzarella cheese and a Riviera vinaigrette; Fritto Misto, breaded fish fingers, baby squid, cracked conch golden fried, served with tartar sauce; Osso Bucco; House Special – Caribbean-style strudel, shrimp and sea scallops in a peppered cheese and herb sauce, rolled in phyllo pastry and served over lobster sauce.

THE DROP OFF PUB, $-$$
Bay Street
☎ *242/322-3444*
Dress code: casual
Reservations: optional

This pub serves English and Bahamian versions of pub grub, from fish 'n chips to peas 'n rice. A favorite with late-night eaters (the kitchen stays open until 6 am) this spot really rocks in the evenings when sports TV and dancing bring in the crowds.

FIVE TWINS, $$$
Atlantis, Paradise Island
☎ *242/636-3000*
Dress code: casually elegant or dressy
Reservations: suggested

This elegant eatery serves up an eclectic menu that features Asian dishes with a gourmet twist.

Five Twins Sample Dinner Menu

☀ APPETIZERS: Pepper-cured salmon served with Dijon and vegetable tempura; chilled oysters with curried haricots vert, apple slaw and sesame lahvosh; spinach salad with potato crisp, wild mushrooms and walnut vinaigrette; tuna ceviche with endive, jicama, macadamia and lemon oil; pumpkin soup with poppy seed and crème fraîche; hearts of palm salad with grilled prawns and sherry vinaigrette.

☀ ENTREES: Sweet and spicy lamb with white beet crudité, red chard and spinach poori; crispy lobster tail with tomato fennel-infused vegetable dressing and soba noodles; steamed seabass with baked eggplant and cardamom-carrot juice; grilled filet of beef with quick-seared bean sprouts in ginger-saffron jus; hot and sour duck breast with rosemary essence, grilled pineapple and sticky rice cake; skewered grilled salmon with tandoori-baked cauliflower and green mango chutney; calamari noodles with wok-charred squid, chorizo and endive; prawn curry with coconut broth, caramelized bok choy and tofu;

The Bahamas

wasabi caviar ravioli with parsnip and celery-ginger jus.

☀ SIDE DISHES: Wok-seared and served family-style for the table: bean sprouts, broccoli, mushrooms, fried noodles and fried rice.

☀ DESSERTS: Assorted sorbets; spiced red berry fusion with sago, almond milk drizzle; tea-infused crème brûlée with coffee mousse and sesame brittle; ginger-scented floating islands with mango broth and gianduja (chocolate-hazelnut) satay sticks; dark and white chocolate dome with gold leaf sake ice cream and hazelnut brittle.

FLAMINGO GARDENS CAFE, $-$$
109 Collins Ave.
☎ *242/356-7904*
Dress code: casual
Reservations: not required

You can eat here or get a carry-out meal for a beachside picnic of crab and rice, boiled chicken, cassava, sweet potato, steamed conch, peas and grits, and other local dishes. Member of A Real Taste of the Bahamas.

THE FORGE, $$$
Radisson Cable Beach
☎ *242/327-6000*
Dress code: casually elegant
Reservations: suggested

Homesick for a little home cooking? Here's your chance to show off your own culinary skills. Guests are seated around a table-top grill and can prepare their own steaks, seafood or chicken.

GAYLORDS, $$-$$$
Dowdeswell Street
☎ *242/356-3004*
Dress code: dress, no casual attire
Reservations: requested

Located in a 150-year-old Bahamian home, Gaylords offers authentic Indian (not West Indian) cuisine. Tandoori and Indian dishes fill the menu. A specialty shop next door sells related food items.

GRAYCLIFF, $$$$
West Hill Street
☎ *242 / 322-2797*
Dress code: dressy, jacket and tie suggested
Reservations: required

The most famous gourmet restaurant in all of The Bahamas (and, some say, the Caribbean), Graycliff has received numerous awards and honors. A member of the Chaîne Des Rôtisseurs, the oldest culinary association in the world founded in 1248 by the king of France, this restaurant is reason enough to schedule a trip to the islands if you are serious about fine dining.

Graycliff is *the* place for visiting celebrities, drawing such stellar diners as Sean Connery, King Constantine, Princess Caroline, Barbara Mandrell, Paul Newman and Stevie Wonder.

The restaurant has also been named one of the world's 10 best restaurants by *Lifestyles of the Rich and Famous*. Other accolades include the Grand Award by *Wine Spectator* for its 180,000-bottle wine cellar. (The award has been bestowed on only 93 restaurants around the world.) A quick look at Graycliff's restaurant verifies the magazine's choice: if you're feeling generous you can order up a bottle of 1865 Château Lafite for $16,000 or 1795 Terrantez for $17,200. The restaurant also features rare cognacs from the Charente region of southwest France, including a 1788 Clos de Giffier Cognac and an 1872 Armagnac Janneau. The restaurant is also noted for having one of the best Cuban cigar collections in the world. The five-star eatery serves gourmet Bahamian and continental dishes at fairly high prices; expect to spend about $150 for dinner for two. Historic Graycliff, on the National Register of Historic Places, is also an inn. Chef Ashwood Darville's specialties include dishes such as Bahamian crawfish in puff pastry, grouper with cream and Dijon mustard (this dish was featured in *Gourmet* magazine), roast rack of lamb marinated in Graycliff's secret recipe, and pepper filet with sweet, hot, white and black peppers, cream, onions, and cognac.

The setting is as exquisite as the cuisine, filled with antique charm and elegance from a Baccarat chandelier to photographs of King George VI at Buckingham Palace. Diners can enjoy their meal in the library dining rooms, filled with rare books.

Grouper Dijonnaise Graycliff, Graycliff

- *2 8-ounce fillets of grouper, skinned*
- *1 large tomato*
- *flour for dredging*
- *¼ cup clarified butter*
- *½ teaspoon minced shallots*
- *1 teaspoon Dijon mustard*
- *¼ cup dry white wine*
- *½ cup heavy cream*
- *¼ teaspoon horseradish*
- *1 teaspoon freshly minced parsley leaves*
- *½ teaspoon paprika*
- *salt and black pepper to taste*

Preheat oven to 425°F. In a saucepan of boiling water, blanch the tomato for about 20 seconds or until the skin begins to peel. Drain, remove the skin and cut the tomato in six slices.

Sprinkle the grouper fillets with salt and pepper and dredge in flour, shaking off the excess. In an oven-proof skillet, sauté fish in butter over moderately high heat. Remove fillets from pan. Drain excess butter from skillet and add shallots. In the meantime, spread ½ teaspoon of mustard on top of each fillet, followed by three tomato slices. Add the wine to shallots in skillet and allow to evaporate to one third of its volume. Add the cream, ½ teaspoon mustard, horseradish, and salt and pepper to taste. Mix well.

Add the fillets to the skillet and bake in the oven for five minutes. Transfer to a heated platter and spoon the sauce over the fish. Garnish by sprinkling the parsley and paprika over the dish. *Serves two.* ☀

Sample Dinner Menu, Graycliff

- HORS-D'OEUVRES: Bahamian lobster in puff pastry with cream and saffron; jumbo shrimp cocktail; éscargots, wild mushrooms with fresh cream and wine; smoked Scottish salmon slices with cream cheese; chef's coquille inspiration; thin slices of beef and fish marinated in a delicate sauce.

- CAVIARS AND TERRINES: Beluga imperial and Russian golden malossol caviar; goose liver pâté with truffles; duck terrine with green peppercorns and cognac.

- SOUPS AND PASTAS: fettuccine with a secret sauce; tortellini with pesto; pasta Graycliff, a light, delicate dish; Bahamian lobster bisque; conch chowder; grandmother's onion soup.

- SALADS: caesar; Graycliff salad with house dressing; goose and shrimp salad with whipped butter and pink berries; Bahamian specialty salad.

- FROM THE GRILL: shrimp and scallops with butter; grilled spiny lobster with two sauces; grilled grouper with drawn butter and leeks; sole filets with champagne butter sauce; Angus prime center cut sirloin steak with mushrooms and Graycliff butter; Angus prime filet mignon with mushrooms and tomatoes.

- ENTREES: medallions of lamb in a delicate Chablis sauce; veal chop with rosemary and wild mushrooms; roast duckling laced in a wild fruit sauce and Grand Marnier; lobster Graycliff, a specialty of the chef; broiled snapper (chef's recipe)

- ENTREES FOR TWO: Angus chateaubriand with Bearnaise sauce; roast rack of lamb; lobster, shrimp, grouper, mushrooms and vegetables.

GREEN SHUTTERS INN, $$-$$$
48 Parliament Street
☎ 242 / 325-5702
Dress code: dressy
Reservations: required

This English pub is located in a Bahamian home that dates back two centuries. Order up British favorites such as fish and chips or steak and kidney pie. Enjoy it all in a delightful pub atmosphere.

GRAYLEATH, All-inclusive
Club Med, Casuarina Drive, Paradise Island
☎ *242/363-2640*
Dress code: dressy
Reservations: required

Diners who aren't guests of Club Med can purchase a night pass to enjoy this candlelit restaurant. After a romantic dinner at this elegant restaurant, sit back and enjoy the Club Med evening entertainment.

Club Med's Codfish Fritters

- *1½ cups flour*
- *½ teaspoon salt*
- *2 eggs*
- *3 tablespoons unsalted butter, melted and cooled*
- *1 cup milk*
- *½ pound codfish*
- *1 fresh hot pepper, seeded*
- *2 green onions, finely chopped*
- *1 clove garlic, crushed*
- *1 tablespoon chopped parsley*
- *¼ teaspoon thyme*
- *dash of allspice*
- *oil for frying*

Sift flour and salt, then beat eggs and butter. Place together in one bowl and add milk, stirring only to mix. (If butter is too stiff, add more milk.) Cover and let stand for two to three hours.

Soak fish in cold water. Drain, remove any bones and skin. Pound fish in a mortar with hot pepper. Add scallions, garlic, parsley, thyme, allspice and pepper to taste. Stir into batter and allow to stand for 30 minutes. Heat oil in deep fryer to 375° and fry mixture by heaped teaspoons until golden brown. Drain on paper towels. *Serves six.* ❧

HOUSE OF WONG, $$
Marlborough Street
☎ 242 / 326-0045
Dress code: casually elegant
Reservations: optional

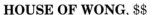Chefs from Hong Kong and New York cook the Chinese dishes here, including specialties like wonton soup and hot and sour soup. Lunch and dinner are served daily. A popular spot for local business people, the House of Wong is a good option when you're ready for a break from seafood.

KINGFISH BLU BAR
AND GRILL AMERICANA, $$
West Bay Street
☎ 242 / 323-2236
Dress code: smart attire after 5 pm
Reservations: suggested

This restaurant offers a little of everything: Tex-Mex, Cajun, steaks, seafood and local selections. Start your evening with a martini (they offer over 20 types!), then dig into sizzling fajitas, a juicy steak or fresh Bahamian lobster. A cigar room is available.

MAMA LIDDY'S PLACE, $
Market Street
☎ 242 / 328-6849
Dress code: casual
Reservations: not required

This Bahamian restaurant has conch chowder, grouper, peas and rice, and other local dishes. The mood is casual and fun. This former Bahamian home is a great place to meet locals. A member of A Real Taste of the Bahamas program.

MAMA LOO'S, $$-$$$
Atlantis, Paradise Island
☎ 242 / 363-3000
Dress code: casually elegant or dressy
Reservations: suggested

A dinner-only eatery where diners are treated to unique Caribbean-Chinese dishes. The restaurant has torchlight chandeliers, rattan wingback chairs and a tropical atmosphere. A favorite with romantics.

MONTAGU GARDENS, $-$$
East Bay Street
(one mile east of the Paradise Island Bridge)
☎ 242/394-6347
Dress code: casually elegant
Reservations: suggested

This elegant restaurant specializes in grilled food, such as blackened grouper, grilled grouper with wine sauce, filet mignon with mushrooms, and more. It's located in a former Bahamian home on Lake Waterloo. A member of A Real Taste of the Bahamas program.

MURRAY'S DELI, $
Atlantis, Paradise Island
☎ 242/636-3000
Dress code: casual
Reservations: not required

Thanks to the new Royal Towers at Atlantis, Nassau now has a genuine deli with decor straight from the '50s – Miami style. Diners are seated in terrazzo booths to enjoy their meal, which is served in generous portions. You can start the day with breakfast or visit later for more serious fare. Late-night dining is another option, with service that continues until 6am. The deli also includes an ice cream parlor with gelato, granita, ice cream, designer sodas, cookies and candies.

Sample Menu, Murray's Deli

❄ BREAKFAST: Mamaliga (as a cereal or lightly fried with sour cream); cheese omelette; matzo brei, pancake style with applesauce; corned beef hash with fried or poached egg; two eggs any style; eggs and lox; smoked salmon platter with bagel, cream cheese, tomato and onion; blintzes with curd cheese and cinnamon sugar, blueberry or strawberry preserve.

❄ APPETIZERS: Gefilte fish made with matzo meal and pike served with horseradish cream; jumbo shrimp cocktail; kasha varnishkas (kasha, egg noodles, onion and beef broth); stuffed cabbage in tomato sauce; potato pancakes with sour cream or applesauce; fried mozzarella sticks with mustard sauce; chopped liver with onions, egg and challah bread.

- FROM THE GRIDDLE: Grilled knockwurst with sauerkraut; Chairman burger with selected spices on kaiser roll; New York-style frankfurter; ranch burger with bacon and swiss cheese; hot roast beef with sweet peppers au jus.

- NEW YORK DELI SANDWICHES: Corned beef, hot pastrami, roast beef, tongue, beef brisket, turkey, hard salami.

- DESSERTS: Atlantis cheesecake with sour cream topping, strawberry or chocolate; Hungarian apple strudel with vanilla sauce and ice cream; carrot cake with cream cheese topping; seven-layer red devil's food cake; jelly roll; Boston cream pie; strawberry shortcake; Black Forest cake; double-double chocolate cake.

PASSIN' JACKS RESTAURANT, $-$$
East Bay Street (¹⁄₂ mile east of the Paradise Island Bridge)
☎ *242 / 394-3245*
Dress code: casually elegant
Reservations: optional

Bahamian specialties (broiled grouper, cracked conch and chowder), as well as American favorites (such as fajitas and steaks) are found at this harborside restaurant. A member of A Real Taste of the Bahamas program. Passin' Jacks offers a real taste of island cuisine in a family-friendly setting.

PLANET HOLLYWOOD, $$
Bay Street at East Street
☎ *242 / 325-STAR*
Dress Code: casual
Reservations: required

Planet Hollywood, with its outrageously high noise level and location-to-location sameness, is definitely not our favorite choice as a dining spot. However, it is popular with many.

THE POOP DECK, $-$$$
East Bay Street, just east of Paradise Island Bridge
☎ 242/393-8175
Dress code: casual
Reservations: optional

This longtime favorite was the first place we ate in The Bahamas many years ago and remains one of our top choices today. Start with a Bahamian cocktail (or select from the extensive wine list), then move on to Bahamian specialties such as conch chowder, grouper fingers, conch salad, cracked conch, Bahamian lobster and more. One of the best places for Bahamian seafood on the island, this family-friendly choice has good views of the water. A member of A Real Taste of the Bahamas program.

THE SHOAL, $-$$
Nassau Street
☎ 242/343-4400
Dress code: casual
Reservations: not required

Dine in or grab a meal to go. This restaurant specializes in Bahamian dishes and is well known for its boiled fish. Other favorites included stewed fish, cracked conch, stewed conch and a special variety platter with conch, shrimp and grouper. A favorite with local families and a member of A Real Taste of the Bahamas program.

SOLE MARE, $$$
Nassau Marriott Resort and Crystal Palace Casino
Cable Beach
☎ 242/327-6200, ext. 6861
Dress code: dressy, jackets required
Reservations: required

Sole Mare serves gourmet Italian fare. It's open for dinner only, Tuesday through Sunday, all served in a classy atmosphere. You'd never guess the casino was just a dice roll away!

SPICES, All-inclusive
Sandals Royal Bahamian Resort And Spa
Cable Beach
☎ 242/327-6400
Dress code: casually elegant
Reservations: suggested

Mediterranean and Caribbean dishes are prepared in an open kitchen at Spices. Start with mussels Provençale, sautéed mussels with white wine, fresh cream, shallots and fresh herbs, or a tasty Mediterranean seafood soup. Entrées include such favorites as grouper Riviera (pan-fried grouper fillet with garlic, olives, capers, tomato and roasted almonds), penne Arrabbiata (penne pasta sautéed with roasted pancetta in a tomato sauce), and veal Valencia (veal scaloppini sautéed in tomato sauce and served with roasted eggplant, fontina cheese and a mushroom coulis. This couples-only option is romantic, with many two-person tables and an intimate atmosphere.

STARS RESTAURANT AND DELI, $-$$
Circle Palm Mall, Soldier Road
☎ 242/394-1692
Dress code: casual
Reservations: not required

You have the option to dine in or take out a picnic of Bahamian seafood, including boiled fish, grouper, peas and grits, fried plantains, chicken, ribs, souse and other delights. A good choice for families. A member of A Real Taste of the Bahamas program.

SUN AND..., $$$
Lakeview Road off Shirley Street
☎ 242/343-2644
Dress code: dressy (jacket and tie preferred, no casual attire)
Reservations: required

Both French and Bahamian dishes are found in this elegant eatery. French dishes include duckling with raspberry sauce, rack of lamb and a selection of soufflés. Bahamian specialties include stone crab and guava duff. The elegant surroundings draw romantic couples looking for a special evening. A member of A Real Taste of the Bahamas program.

TEQUILA PEPE'S STEAKHOUSE, $$-$$$
Radisson Cable Beach
☎ 242/327-6000
Dress code: casually elegant
Reservations: suggested

This place holds the title as the only Mexican restaurant in The Bahamas. As you probably guessed, margaritas and Mexican dishes highlight the offerings, all served in a festive atmosphere decorated with oversized cacti, sombreros and piñatas. As Texans and big fans of Tex-Mex cuisine, we felt we had to give it a try, and we were pleasantly surprised to find such excellent fare in the islands, from enchiladas to tacos.

TOI ET MOI, $$$
Harbour Bay Shopping Centre, East Bay Street
☎ 242/394-7056
Dress code: dressy
Reservations: suggested

French food is the specialty – black truffles, foie gras, smoked salmon. Also served are Bahamian favorites prepared with a French flair. The restaurant offers a good wine list as well as selections of aged Cognacs, Armagnacs and Calvados. The atmosphere is romantic – save this one for a special celebration.

TONY ROMA'S, $-$$
West Bay Street (opposite Saunders Beach), Cable Beach
☎ 242/325-2020
Dress code: casually elegant
Reservations: optional

Along with traditional Tony Roma's fare such as baby back ribs and barbecue, this location serves up Bahamian conch chowder, conch fritters, cracked conch and other local favorites. Just like its Stateside properties, this Tony Roma's has a casual, family-friendly atmosphere. A member of A Real Taste of the Bahamas program.

TRAVELERS REST, $-$$
West Bay Street, Gambier (one mile west of Airport Road)
☎ *242/327-7633*
www.travelersrest.com
Dress code: casually elegant
Reservations: Optional

☀ This restaurant calls itself the home of the banana dai-
quiri, but it's also known for its Bahamian menu: minced
crawfish, grouper, conch and guava cake. This is a good choice
if you want to try some Bahamian delights. The atmosphere
is relaxed, with umbrella-shaded tables tucked beneath tall
palms. A member of A Real Taste of the Bahamas program,
the restaurant is located west of Cable Beach.

Where To Stay

ATLANTIS, PARADISE ISLAND, $$
Paradise Island
☎ *800/321-3000, 242/363-3000, fax 242/363-2493*

☀ This resort truly transforms Paradise Island into Fantasy Island. Along with an elegant hotel, it brings to The
Bahamas a water park that's unequaled in the Caribbean.
You can walk through a 100-foot-long clear tunnel, surrounded by thousands of tropical fish, sharks, manta rays
and sea turtles in the world's largest open-air aquarium.
From above, a lagoon bar and several bridges look down on
these denizens of the deep.

The tunnel and the 14-acre water gardens surrounding it are
the kind of place travelers either love or hate. Don't expect to
find peace and quiet here, or even a Caribbean atmosphere.
This is Vegas-goes-to-the-beach, but if you're into non-stop
fun it's the place to be on Paradise Island.

Atlantis is a fantasy vacation resort with pleasures for children (of which you'll see many) and adults.

There are numerous dining choices here, including fine dining at the Bahamian Club steakhouse. Other options are

Mama Loo's Chinese restaurant and Villa d'Este, a trattoria specializing in Northern Italian cuisine.

Caribbean Seafood Strudel in Mango-Lime Sauce, Atlantis

Seafood Strudel:

- *olive oil*
- *½ pound grouper*
- *8 large shrimp, peeled and deveined*
- *⅓ pound scallops*
- *1 lobster tail*
- *salt and pepper to taste*
- *1 onion, sliced*
- *shrimp and lobster shells*
- *1 tablespoon tomato paste*
- *1 cup sherry*
- *2 cups whipping cream*
- *¼ cup chopped basil*
- *½ cup grated Parmesan cheese*
- *½ cup breadcrumbs*
- *6 sheets phyllo dough layered with melted butter*

In a very hot oiled pan, separately sear the grouper, shrimp, scallops and lobster tail, seasoned with salt and pepper. Cool and drain, then dice. Sauté onion, shrimp and lobster shells in oil. Add tomato paste and sherry. Cover. Add the cream and cook until thickened. Strain over seafood. Add basil, cheese and breadcrumbs. Cool.

Preheat the oven to 375°F. Place the seafood mixture on the phyllo sheets and roll into a log. Fold the ends so the mixture cannot leak out. Bake on parchment paper for 15 minutes or until browned.

Mango-Lime Sauce:

- *2 mangoes, peeled, pitted and diced*
- *1 cup pineapple juice*
- *¼ cup lime juice (or to taste)*

Bring all the ingredients to a boil. Strain.

Slice the seafood strudel and serve with the mango-lime sauce. *Makes four servings.* ☀

HILTON BRITISH COLONIAL, $$
1 Bay Street, Nassau
☎ *242/322-3301, fax 242/322-2286*

This historic hotel sits at the head of Bay Street, a reminder of Nassau's early hotel days. It's a warm reminder of our early hotel days as well, as the scene of our first visit to the Caribbean.

The British Colonial (or BC, as the taxi drivers say) was looking a bit worn, but we're happy to say a major renovation recently transformed the tired hotel into one of Nassau's most sought addresses. Today, it offers 291 rooms with satellite TV, desk, modem outlet, mini-bar, voice mail and more. Business and executive floors are available. Guests can enjoy the small beach, health club, dive shop and four restaurants.

BREEZES BAHAMAS, $
Cable Beach
☎ *800/859-SUPER, 242/327-6153; fax 242/327-5155*
www.breezes.com

This may just be the all-inclusive bargain of the Caribbean. Part of the SuperClubs chain, Breezes is a moderately-priced property. Unlike the sprawling resorts of the chain, the Breezes properties (there are two Breezes in The Bahamas) are somewhat smaller and charge a fee for some premium activities. But it does offer all the amenities of the SuperClubs chain, including excellent meals (one of our tastiest meals in Nassau was a buffet lunch at this property), watersports, bars and nightclubs, and even free weddings.

This 400-room resort emphasizes fun and relaxation. The decor is bright and tropical, from its open-air lobby to the rooms to the lemon-yellow exterior. No one under 16 is permitted in this singles and couples resort.

CLUB MED PARADISE ISLAND, $$
Paradise Island
☎ *800/CLUB MED, 242/363-2640, fax 242/363-3496*
www.clubmed.com

This recently renovated property offers not only double rooms with one queen or two twin beds, but also a two-story villa called House in the Woods, which has a living room with television and stereo, fully equipped and stocked kitchenette, bedroom with queen-size bed, wrap-around porches, and more.

The villa was built as a set for the 1978 movie *Le Sauvage* starring Yves Montand and Catherine Deneuve. It was later brought to Paradise Island and renovated. Three restaurants are located on property and guests enjoy a full menu of activity as well: billiards, deep-sea fishing, fitness center, golf, kayaking, sailing, scuba diving, 18 Har-Tru tennis court and windsurfing. All ages are welcomed at this property, although special children's programs are not offered.

Club Med's Chocolate Bread

- *35 ounces flour*
- *19½ ounces cold water*
- *¾ ounces salt*
- *¾ ounces butter*
- *7 ounces chocolate chunks*

Knead the flour and water for 10 minutes. Add salt and butter, then chocolate. Distribute into three pans (17.5 ounces each) and cook in a 240° oven for 25 minutes.

Club Med Shrimp and Crabmeat Canapes

- *50 snow peas*
- *8 quarts water*
- *½ pound lump crabmeat, well drained*
- *¼ baby shrimp, chopped*
- *½ large red pepper, finely diced*
- *4 celery stalks, diced*
- *2 tablespoons parsley, chopped*
- *¼ cup mayonnaise*
- *5 tablespoons lemon juice*
- *salt and pepper to taste*

Blanch snow peas in salted boiling water. Plunge into cold water, pat dry, and set aside.

Mix remaining ingredients and toss lightly. Salt and pepper to taste.

Open pea pods and with a fork and place a teaspoon of mixture into the cavity. Carefully wipe the outside of pods.

Line the filled pods in a flat pan with dry paper towels. Chill until ready to serve. ☀

■ ■

COMFORT SUITES, $$
Paradise Island Drive
Paradise Island
☎ *800-228-5150, 242/363-3680, fax 242/363-2588*

This 150-room hotel is an economical choice on Paradise island. Rooms include a complimentary continental breakfast daily, and guests have full signing privileges at Atlantis restaurants.

COMPASS POINT, $$-$$$$
Compass Point Beach
☎ *800/OUTPOST, 242/327-4500, fax 242/327-3299*
www.islandoutpost.com

You won't find many resorts that list "state-of-the-art re-cording studio" among their features, but here's one, thanks to owner Chris Blackwell. The creator of Island Records has a string of small, fine hotels in the Caribbean, including Jamaica and Young Island in St. Vincent and the Grenadines.

Compass Point is about 25 minutes west of Nassau, set away from the casinos and mega-resorts of Cable Beach on a quiet stretch of the island near the upscale Lyford Cay, where stellar residents such as Sean Connery and Mick Jagger have residences in the private no-visitors-allowed compound. You might get lucky and spot a familiar face at Compass Point, as there's a dock for Lyford Cay residents.

Compass Point has only 18 rooms, but you can't miss this rainbow property. Look for the festive colors of the Junkanoo festival: vibrant tones of purple, blue, yellow and red. Each individual cottage is decorated in a style that might be described as Caribbean kitsch meets "Gilligan's Island." Guests can choose from five cabana rooms (the only air-conditioned accommodations) or the larger, more private huts and cottages (which include a downstairs open-air kitchen and picnic-table dining room). Every room is filled hand-crafted furniture and faces the sea. End your day in the rocking chairs on your private porch that looks out to the sea, then come in to sleep beneath a ceiling fan in a hand-made bed covered with a Bahamian batik spread.

After a day on the beach, you can enjoy a casually elegant meal in the resort restaurant. The Californian-Caribbean cuisine offered here draws both with hotel guests and locals.

Compass Point.

GRAYCLIFF HOTEL, $$-$$$$
West Hill Street
☎ *242/322-2796, fax 242/326-6110*
www.graycliff.com

☀This historic building is situated next to Government House and offers 13 luxurious guest accommodations and spacious pool cottage suites. This building dates back to Nassau's swashbuckling days. The mansion was originally built by Captain John Howard Graysmith, a pirate who commanded the schooner *Graywold* and plundered treasure ships along the Spanish Main. In 1776, the mansion became the headquarters for the American Navy when Nassau was captured by the soldiers. In 1844, Graycliff became Nassau's first inn.

The home has a rich history of celebrity visitors. During Prohibition, Graycliff was owned by Mrs. Polly Leach, a companion to Al Capone. Later, Graycliff was purchased by Lord and Lady Dudley, Third Earl of Staffordshire, who hosted many dignitaries including the Duke and Duchess of Windsor, Lord Beaverbrook, Lord Mountbatten and Sir Winston Churchill. In 1973 Enrico and Anna Maria Garzaroli purchased Graycliff and turned the mansion into a hotel and restaurant.

Guests can choose from old or new decor. Those with a flair for historic furnishings will like the Pool Cottage, where Winston Churchill used to stay, or the Baillou, the original master bedroom in the main house. Travelers with a taste for modern decor find it in the Mandarino Cottage, which has an extra large bathroom and whirlpool tub. All rooms are air-conditioned and have a private bath. Breakfast is served to hotel guests only. The hotel is planning an expansion that will include eight additional guest rooms and two swimming pools.

NASSAU MARRIOTT RESORT AND CRYSTAL PALACE CASINO, $$
Cable Beach
☎ *800/222-7466, 242/327-6200, fax 242/327-6801*
www.marriott.com

⋮●⋮Cable Beach's largest hotel is tough to miss. The 867-room property literally glows in the dark, with colored lights over each balcony giving the hotel the look of a seaside candy cane. This is one of the liveliest nightspots in town, thanks to its super-sized casino and glitzy revue.

THE OCEAN CLUB, $$-$$$$+
Paradise Island Drive
Paradise Island
☎ *800/321-3000, 242/363-3000, fax 242/363-3703*
E-mail: wpearce@pid.sunint.com

This ultra-elegant resort is the stuff of the rich and famous. Cindy Crawford was married here a few years ago and the small resort received worldwide attention, but the well-heeled have been coming here for many years. The resort has entertained Ronald Reagan, Sean Connery, Michael Caine, Sidney Poitier, Magic Johnson and many other celebrities.

The estate was first named Shangri-la and was purchased in 1962 by Huntington Hartford, heir to the Great Atlantic and Pacific Tea Company fortune. The estate had formal Versailles-inspired gardens and statues of Napoleon's Josephine, FDR, David Livingstone and more. Huntington built a 51-room resort and restaurant and renamed what was then Hog Island as Paradise Island.

In 1994, Sun International (the same company that owns Atlantis as well as South Africa's Sun City) purchased Ocean Club and totally renovated the resort. The hotel now offers 71 guest rooms, including four suites and five two-bedroom villas, each with a private whirlpool. All accommodations in the main building have central air-conditioning, indoor ceiling fans, outdoor ceiling fans on balconies or patios, mini-bars, safes, and 27-inch televisions.

At time of press, this hotel was undergoing renovation, so you can expect it be even better in the future.

RADISSON CABLE BEACH, $$
Cable Beach
☎ *800/333-3333, 242/327-6000, fax 242/327-6987*
www.radisson.com/nassaubs_cable

This beachfront resort boasts numerous restaurants in its all-inclusive plan. "Recognizing that guests have different tastes, we have designed our all-inclusive vacation to include extensive dining options," said Brian Meister, vice president of sales and marketing for the 700-room resort. Options include The Bimini Market Grill for casual dining and breakfast buffets, The Amici Restaurant for Italian fare, the Dolphin Grill for light lunches, Avocado's for fine dining, and The Forge for steaks and grilled fare.

Sporting a new $15 million renovation, the Radisson Cable Beach offers round-the-clock action both on and off the beach. Every room in the high-rise hotel has an ocean view.

> ☀ *TIP: For real luxury, splurge to stay in one of the junior suites located at the end of each floor. We did, and we enjoyed sunrise from the bedroom balcony and sunset from the living room balcony.*

A shopping arcade (with surprisingly good prices, we found) connects the Radisson with the Marriott Crystal Palace Casino.

The hotel's all-inclusive program, Splash, is available for less than $100 per person, per day. Participants wear a wristband that allows them unlimited use of all sports, plus all meals, drinks and snacks. The plan also includes all tips.

Minced Lobster, Radisson Cable Beach

- *3 8-ounce lobster tails*
- *4 ounces onion, julienned*
- *4 ounces celery, julienned*
- *4 ounces green sweet pepper, julienned*
- *4 ounces tomato paste*
- *salt/pepper to taste*
- *sprig thyme*
- *2 ounces oil*

Boil lobster tail and allow to cool. Split tails and remove trail. Loosely pick lobster meat. In frying pan, heat oil. Add onions, peppers and celery, then stir until translucent.

Add tomatoes and thyme and allow to cook for three minutes. Add the lobster meat and tomato paste. Mix well and cook on high for two minutes. Reduce heat and allow to simmer for 10 minutes. Moisten with a little fish stock or water if necessary. Serve with peas 'n rice, vegetables and fried plantains.

Serving tip: Minced lobster can also be used to fill spring rolls. Take one package of spring roll wrappers and fill each with one ounce of minced lobster. Roll tightly into cylindrical shape. Moisten edge with beaten egg. Deep-fry until golden brown. Serve hot. Mango chutney makes an excellent dip. ☀

■ ■

SANDALS ROYAL BAHAMIAN RESORT AND SPA, $$
Cable Beach
☎ *800/SANDALS, 242/327-6400, fax 242/327-6961*
www.sandals.com

This Sandals offers couples a romantic, elegant atmosphere with all the options of the all-inclusives. Along with a full menu of watersports fun, a highlight of this resort is its excellent spa. Guests can purchase spa treatments à la carte or in packages, selecting from facials, massages, body scrubs, aromatherapy and reflexology services. Also available are manicures, pedicures, paraffin hand and foot treatments, and more.

Spicy Jerk Chicken Chili, Sandals Resorts

- *5 ounces boneless cubed chicken*
- *1 ounce Walkers Wood jerk seasoning*
- *½ teaspoon finely chopped garlic*
- *1 ounce small diced, seeded tomatoes*
- *1 teaspoon chopped scallion*
- *1 ounce chopped onions*
- *3 ounces chicken stock*
- *½ ounce diced carrots*
- *½ ounce cooked red beans*
- *1 teaspoon vegetable oil*
- *½ teaspoon crushed pimento berries (allspice)*
- *1 teaspoon tomato paste*

Heat oil in saucepan. Add chicken and sauté until lightly brown. Add jerk seasonings. Add scallion, onions, tomato, garlic, carrots, beans and pimento berries, and continue to sauté. Add tomato paste and incorporate well. Add stock and cook for 25 minutes. ❀

■ ■ ■ ■ ■ ■ ■ ■ ■ ■ ■ ■ ■ ■ ■ ■ ■ ■ ■ ■

Sandals Resorts takes their food as seriously as their fun and has retained the services of food consultant and renowned restaurateur Walter Staib. Founder of the Caribbean Hotel Association's Caribbean Culinary Awards of Excellence and the first inductee into the Caribbean Culinary Hall of Fame, Staib is considered one of the foremost experts on interpreting, creating and promoting the ingredients and qualities of Caribbean cuisine.

"We are delighted to have Walter on our team," said Gordon "Butch" Stewart, chairman of the Sandals Resorts International. "He [Staib] has devoted his life to the selection, preparation and presentation of fine food. His extraordinary talent will help Sandals as we continue on the path of providing the most luxurious resort experience, of which dining is an essential element."

Staib began his culinary career at the age of 14 and received formal training in Europe. In 1989 he launched Concepts by Staib, Ltd., a hospitality consulting firm. Staib has been awarded the prestigious Chevalier de L'Ordre du Merite Agricole de la République Française in recognition of his dedication to the advancement of the restaurant industry and received the Silver Plate, the restaurant and hospitality industry's highest honor. His flagship restaurant is The City Tavern in Philadelphia, a recreation of an 18th-century public house.

SOUTH OCEAN GOLF AND BEACH RESORT, $$
South Ocean
☎ *800/252-7466, 242/362-4391, fax 242/362-4310*

For real peace and quiet, this is the place to come on New Providence. Located by itself on a wide swath of beach, this property is ideal for travelers who don't want the hustle

and bustle of shops and casinos (or who are content with taking the hotel van to Nassau for a day of activity).

Accommodations include rooms in the main house and some
on the beach (our choice). They are decorated with Caribbean
furnishings and pencil post beds, and have balconies or patios
that look directly out to the shallow sea.

Between Meals

Nassau is filled with more activity options than any
other Bahamian destination. The heart of Nassau is
Rawson Square. Make your first stop here at the Visitors
Information Center for brochures and maps before starting
off on busy **Bay Street**, the shopping district. Here, gold and
gems are sold alongside straw baskets and T-shirts at the
Straw Market, one of the most popular souvenir stops.

The bustling Straw Market in Nassau.

Be sure to look behind the Straw Market for a glimpse at the cruise ships that dock at Prince George Dock. At Rawson Square, horse-drawn carriages wait for passengers, who pay $10 (be prepared to negotiate) for a two-person, half-hour ride along picturesque Bay Street.

Parliament House, Nassau.

Ardastra Gardens And Zoo
Chippingham Rd. off West Bay Street
☎ 242/323-5806
Hours: 9 am to 4:30 pm daily
Admission: fee
Another popular attraction is the Ardastra Gardens and Zoo. The only zoo in the Bahamas, Ardastra features 300 species of animals and 50 species of birds, including monkeys, iguanas and marching pink flamingos. Stop here if you have time, but we felt that this is one stop that can be cut from busy itineraries. The caged animals are depressing to view, and we found the personnel here far from friendly.

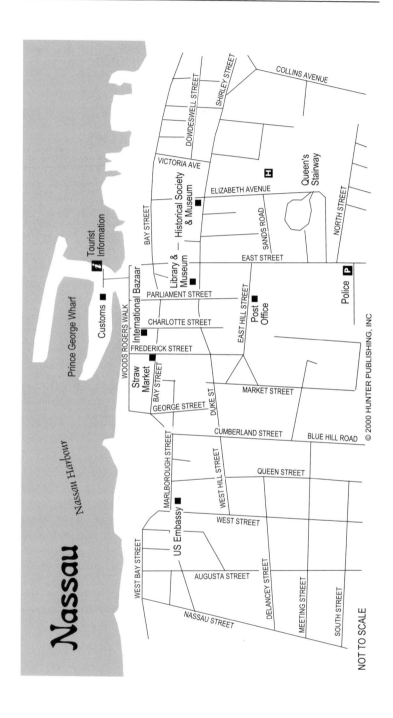

Nassau

Nassau Harbour

Prince George Wharf

Tourist Information

Customs ■

WOODS ROGERS WALK

Straw Market ■

BAY STREET

International Bazaar ■

Library & Museum ■

Historical Society & Museum ■

BAY STREET

VICTORIA AVE

DOWDESWELL STREET

SHIRLEY STREET

COLLINS AVENUE

ELIZABETH AVENUE

Queen's Stairway

NORTH STREET

SANDS ROAD

EAST STREET

H

PARLIAMENT STREET

CHARLOTTE STREET

FREDERICK STREET

EAST HILL STREET

Post Office ■

Police ■ P

GEORGE STREET

DUKE ST

MARKET STREET

CUMBERLAND STREET

BLUE HILL ROAD

MARLBOROUGH STREET

WEST HILL STREET

QUEEN STREET

US Embassy ■

WEST STREET

WEST BAY STREET

AUGUSTA STREET

DELANCEY STREET

MEETING STREET

SOUTH STREET

NASSAU STREET

© 2000 HUNTER PUBLISHING, INC

NOT TO SCALE

Blue Lagoon Island
☎ 242/363-3577
Hours: daily
Admission: yes
One of the most popular activities in Nassau is a day at Blue Lagoon Island. This "uninhabited" island lies about half an hour from the dock at Paradise Island and offers some beautiful beaches, hammocks beneath towering palms and plenty of watersports. For additional charges, visitors can parasail, swim with stingrays or meet dolphins (make reservations early for this choice). One option includes feeding, petting and swimming with the friendly mammals. (The dolphin encounters can also be booked as a separate attraction without a day at Blue Lagoon Island by calling ☎ 242/363-1653.) Blue Lagoon Island is only for those looking to party, not for peace and quiet or anything resembling privacy. If you do make this trip, bring a towel and, to save money, your own snorkel gear.

Botanical Gardens
Chippingham Road off West Bay Street
Hours: 9-4:30 weekdays, 9-4 weekends
Admission: yes
A better choice for those who relish quiet is the nearby Botanical Gardens, where you can walk hand-in-hand along blooming paths that feature tropical plants and flowers.

Changing of the Guard Ceremony
Government House, Blue Hill Road
(5 minutes from downtown)
☎ 242/322-2020
Hours: Every other week at 10 am (call for dates)
Admission: free
Just as at Buckingham Palace, the guards at Government House, representatives of Queen Elizabeth II, change shifts to the full flurry of pomp and circumstance. The Royal Bahamas Police Force Band performs at this event, which is a must-see if you're in the area on the right day.

Fort Charlotte
Off West Bay Street
Hours: Daily (call ahead)
☎ *242/322-7500*
History lovers should head over to Fort Charlotte for a free guided tour of the largest fort in the Bahamas. Perched high on a hill overlooking Cable Beach, this fort never saw action, but sees plenty of activity today as tourists come to enjoy a bird's eye view and a look at dungeons, cannons and some exhibits.

People-to-People
☎ *242/326-5371, 242/328-7810, fax 242/356-0434*
The People-To-People program is an excellent way to learn more about Bahamian residents and culture. This program matches vacationers with more than 1,500 Bahamian volunteers for a day of activities that might include shopping at a local market, dinner with a local family, fishing, boating or a tour of back street sights.

The People-To-People Tea Party is held monthly from 4-5 pm; call for specific dates. Admission is free. People meet at the Government House Ballroom for this special event. Reservations are required so check with your hotel or call the People-to-People Department at the Ministry of Tourism (above). Proper attire is required.

Pompey Museum
Bay Street, Nassau
Hours: 10-4:30 Monday to Friday, 10-1 Saturday
Admission: donation
This museum has many interesting exhibits on the emancipation of enslaved people of The Bahamas.

The Retreat
Village Road
☎ *242/393-1317*
Hours: Tours at 11:45, Tuesday through Thursday
Admission: fee
The Retreat is the home of the Bahamas National Trust. An excellent stop for nature lovers, the site offers guided tours of native plants.

⚘ Shows

Cabaret shows are found at the **Nassau Marriott Resort, the Crystal Palace Casino** (☎ 242/327-6200) and at the **Atlantis Showroom** in the Atlantis Resort on Paradise Island (☎ 242/363-3000).

If you're looking for something more Bahamian, check out the **Kings and Knights Club** (☎ 242/327-7711) at the Forte Nassau Beach Hotel on Cable Beach. For over 35 years, this delightful showplace has entertained visitors with Bahamian songs, dances, steel bands, fire eaters, limbo dancers, comedians and even a few bawdy calypso singers.

Working Off Those Meals

⚘ Golf

There are several courses on the island.

South Ocean Golf Course, ☎ 800/223-6510 or 242/362-4391, was designed by Joe Lee. Par 72, 18 holes.

Cable Beach Golf Course, ☎ 800/451-3103 or 242/327-6000, was designed by Jim McCormick. Par 72, 18 holes. Built in 1929.

The Bahamas

San Salvador

☀ Most regard San Salvador as the site where Christopher Columbus first made landfall in the New World. When he landed (and exactly *where* is also up for debate, although most say Long Bay, at a site now marked with a large stone cross), he found an island named "Guanahani," inhabited by the Lucayan Indians. The explorer renamed the tiny isle San Salvador, or "Holy Savior."

The island became a lot less holy when notorious pirate Captain John Watling decided to set up camp here and proclaim the island his headquarters. The English buccaneer used the island as a hideaway during the 17th century, but Watling's influence long outlived him, and the island took on the name Watling's Island. In 1925 the name of San Salvador was restored.

San Salvador is 200 miles east-southeast of Nassau, southeast of Cat Island. It is a favorite with scuba divers, offering visibility of up to 150 feet. The pace here remains quiet and relaxed. Most activity takes place in **Cockburn** (pronounced KOH-burn) Town, a small community on the west coast.

Where To Stay

CLUB MED-COLUMBUS ISLE, $$
Cockburn Town
☎ *800/CLUB MED, 242/331-2000, fax 242/331-2222*

☀ This all-inclusive resort is a favorite with travelers of all ages, although there are no special facilities for children. The 90-acre resort sprawls along a white sand beach and includes plenty of opportunities for activity: aerobics, bocce ball, deep-sea fishing, horseback riding, kayaking, sailing, snorkeling, scuba diving, softball, soccer, tennis, waterskiing,

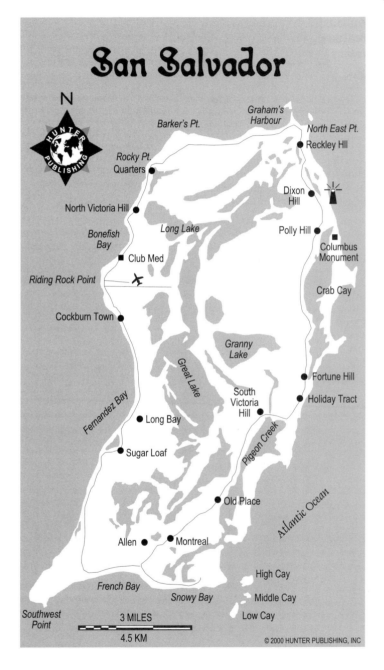

The Bahamas

San Salvador

N

Barker's Pt.

Graham's Harbour

North East Pt.

Reckley Hll

Rocky Pt. Quarters

Dixon Hill

North Victoria Hill

Long Lake

Polly Hill

Bonefish Bay

Columbus Monument

Club Med

Riding Rock Point

Crab Cay

Cockburn Town

Granny Lake

Great Lake

South Victoria Hill

Fortune Hill

Holiday Tract

Fernandez Bay

Long Bay

Pigeon Creek

Sugar Loaf

Atlantic Ocean

Old Place

Allen Montreal

High Cay

French Bay

Snowy Bay

Middle Cay

Southwest Point

3 MILES

Low Cay

4.5 KM

© 2000 HUNTER PUBLISHING, INC

fing, you name it. A spa offers massage and beauty
nts. The resort is a colorful contrast to the turquoise
with yellow, pink and green cottages trimmed in gin-
ad, each with a private balcony or patio.

Club Med Shrimp Cocktail

Shrimp:

- *1 pound shrimp*
- *1 crab boil packet*

Sauce:

- *1 medium onion, chopped*
- *1 garlic clove, crushed*
- *1½ teaspoons lemon juice*
- *1½ cups mayonnaise*
- *2 tablespoons ketchup*
- *½ teaspoon Tabasco sauce*
- *¾ teaspoon Worcestershire sauce*

To prepare shrimp, boil them with crab boil packet until
pink. (The local grocery store will have the crab packet in
the spice section.) Rinse with cold water and chill. Peel
shrimp, leaving tail.

To prepare sauce, mix all ingredients together and chill.
Serve shrimp with sauce. ☀

Between Meals

Dixon Hill Lighthouse
Rum Cay
This 1887 lighthouse is hand-operated, and is one of the last
of its kind in the world. Visitors can climb the steep, winding
stairs to the summit for a wonderful view of the surrounding
waters, up to 19 miles on a clear day. To climb the lighthouse,
stop at the nearby caretaker's cottage.

Farquharson Plantation or Blackbeard's Castle
Pigeon Creek
This site contains the most famous plantation ruins in The Bahamas. They're locally called Blackbeard's Castle because it is rumored that the legendary pirate once stayed here.

People-to-People
☎ *242/326-5371, 242/328-7810, 242/356-0435-8, fax 242/356-0434*
For details on this unique program, see pages 24-26.

Working Off Those Meals

⁘ Scuba Diving

Excellent scuba diving sites are found around San Salvador, including reef and wreck dives at High Cay, Low Cay and Middle Cay. For more information on diving, contact the Bahamas Tourism Board at ☎ 800/8-BAHAMAS.

The Bahamas

Festivals

For information on all the Bahamian festivals listed below, contact the Bahamas Tourism Board at ☎ 212/758-2777, 800/8-BAHAMAS (toll-free) or 800/677-3777 (Canada).

☼ January

New Year's Day Junkanoo Parade, Nassau. This is the biggest blowout of the year. The national party celebrates Junkanoo, a day that brings together Carnival and Mardi Gras with brilliant costumes and a fun atmosphere. The air is filled with the sounds of cowbells, goatskin drums and whistles. Purchase local foods as you watch the parade go by. Junkanoo dates back to the island's slavery days, when slaves were permitted to celebrate Christmas in traditional African style. This fun time starts on Boxing Day (December 26th) and continues until New Year's Day.

Junkanoo

No one quite knows the origin of the word "Junkanoo." Some believe it came from John Canoe, an African leader who demanded the right for slaves to celebrate. Other people believe the term stems from a Scottish saying that the parades were "junk enough."

☼ February

Festival in the Dark. This Nassau event is sponsored by the Ministry of Youth, Sports and Culture. It brings together local music such as rake 'n scrape, with limbo dancing, fire dancing and drumming. Local foods are sold.

Farmer's Cay Festival, Exuma. This event is an annual homecoming for the people of Farmer's Cay, Exuma. You can catch a boat from Nassau to the excursion. Local foods sold.

Ministry of Health Food Fair, Eleuthera. This unique event was the brainchild of a local doctor who started the fair as a fundraising event. Both locals and vacationers attend the international food fair.

❖ March

Heritage Day, Abaco. This Hope Town festival starts with a treasure hunt. It also includes lunch at Jarrett Park, where you can try some local specialties, including conch fritters.

Pineapple Arts Festival, Eleuthera. The famous pineapples of Eleuthera are showcased at this annual event, along with arts and crafts, basketry, paintings and plenty of local food. Bring along your appetite and try some local pastries, preserves and other culinary items.

❖ May

Bahamas Heritage Festival, Nassau. Part of the Great Bahamas Seafood Festival, this cultural event includes traditional music and foods.

❖ June

Pineapple Festival, Eleuthera. This early June event revolves around the pineapples of Eleuthera. There are pineapple recipe contests, pineapple farm tours, crafts, a Junkanoo parade, dances and a pineathalon, which includes a swim, run and bike ride. For information, contact the Eleuthera Tourist Office, ☎ 242/332-2142; fax 242/332-2480.

⁙ July

Regatta Time in Abaco, Abaco. This annual event, now over two decades in existence, includes nine days of boat races, beach picnics, cocktail parties and more.

Beer Festival, Exuma. Held on the full moon, this celebration honors, well, beer.

⁙ August

Staniel Cay Homecoming and Bonefishing Tournament, Exuma. This three-day event pits the anglers against the wrestling bonefish and is scheduled for the first weekend in August. Events include an all-day native food feast.

Emancipation Day, Islands of the Bahamas. Throughout the islands, this public holiday (the first Monday in August) commemorates the emancipation of slavery in 1834. In Nassau, events start with an early morning Junkanoo parade and continue with an afternoon of local foods.

Coca-Cola Bash, Grand Bahama Island. This Emancipation Day event on Grand Bahama Island brings together Bahamian music, local musicians and plenty of local food.

Fox Hill Day Celebration, Nassau. This event takes place a week after Emancipation Day because the residents of Fox Hill didn't learn of the proclamation for one week. Events begin with gospel concerts in local churches followed by an afternoon of local foods. Held the second Tuesday in August in Freedom Park, Fox Hill.

⁙ October

International Month, Nassau. The International Cultural Committee of the Ministry of Foreign Affairs organizes this special event. It features arts, crafts, parades and international foods.

North Eleuthera Sailing Regatta, Eleuthera. Locally built boats from throughout the Islands of the Bahamas take part in this well-known race. Other events include music, road races and plenty of local foods.

McClean's Town Conch Cracking Contest, Grand Bahama Island. How many conch can the conch cracker crack? This fishing village comes to life with plenty of fun on the day of this special event.

Wine and Art Festival, Nassau. This annual event showcases local artists. Enjoy their work while you sample imported wines.

☼ November

Christmas Jollification, Nassau. Shoppers can eye local arts and crafts as well as local holiday foods at this annual event.

Authentically Bahamian Trade Show, Nassau. The Ministry of Tourism organizes this annual event that showcases all kinds of locally made goods, including condiments.

☼ December

Boxing Day Junkanoo Parade, Islands of the Bahamas. Won't be here for the Junkanoo parade on New Year's Day? This parade is an earlier version and takes place on Boxing Day (December 26), a day when the English originally "boxed" Christmas leftovers for servants.

Turks
& Caicos

Introduction

The Turks and Caicos (pronounced CAY-cos) Islands are located 1½ hours from Miami, tucked halfway between the tip of Florida and Puerto Rico. This British crown colony, ruled by a governor appointed by the Queen, is better known to the world of banking than it is to travelers. Its tax-free status, as well as use of the English language and the US dollar as the official currency, have made the Turks and Caicos a popular offshore banking center for American corporations for many years.

We found that the same attributes that make these islands so attractive to businesses also make them appealing to travelers. A journey to the islands is quick, thanks to daily jet service from Miami. Once there, travel around the islands is easy (despite being on the left side of the road). You don't even need to deal with a foreign currency or exchange rate. The political stability of the government has brought a sense of security to the Turks and Caicos. Beaches are safe and uncrowded and tourists can enjoy late-night walks from property to property on the beaches of the main island, Providenciales.

Geography

☀ Although the chain is composed of nearly 40 limestone islands, only eight are considered tourist destinations. **Providenciales**, or Provo, is home to about 6,000 residents and to most of the tourist industry. The capital of the Turks and Caicos is the island of **Grand Turk**, a short hop from Provo. This seven-mile-square island has some historic buildings and the national museum, a must-see for history buffs.

Other inhabited islands include **North Caicos**, the most verdant island in the chain; **South Caicos**, a fishing center; **Middle Caicos**, home of several sea caves; and **Salt Cay**, a tiny island of only 300 residents that was once the world's largest producer of sea salt.

The future of tourism in the Turks and Caicos Islands is easily summed up by the Honorable Oswald Skippings, Minister of Tourism: "We are on a roll." Statistics back up that claim. Visitor arrivals soared to 100,000 in 1997, and those numbers were up 27% for the first quarter of 1998. Construction projects dot the islands, especially on Providenciales. Predictions call for even more promotion of tourism. Upcoming plans will focus not just on Providenciales but on the Turks and Caicos as a whole. "We have eight wonderful inhabited islands and we tend to forget that Providenciales is not the only one," said Caesar Campbell, Director of Tourism.

Plans call for development on many of the outlying areas. East Caicos will be the recipient of one of the largest projects, a $350 million development that will include a cruise port large enough to accommodate up to eight ships. Plans call for the now uninhabited island to offer a five-star hotel, water sports center and golf course. The site is set for a grand opening on New Year's Eve, 2000.

Long-term plans for East Caicos include construction of seven additional resorts on the island's north shore. "We are not looking to develop mass tourism," said Skippings. "The government's aim is to create sustainable tourism and promote growth that is sensitive to and in harmony with the environment."

For now, however, the Turks and Caicos are uncrowded with either residents or tourists. Just how uncrowded these islands are is very obvious when arriving in Providenciales, better known as Provo. Although this island boasts the largest portion of the Turks and Caicos population of 15,000, it is still very open and largely unsettled. The sickle-shaped island is dotted with scrubby growth, short palms and climbing sea grapes. Chalky limestone roads wind across its flatness, connecting settlements like Blue Hills and The Bight.

But the traveler to Provo will soon realize that its desert terrain is just a backdrop for the beaches and clear waters that are the main attractions. On some parts of the island the beaches stretch for miles, dotted with only the footprints of iguanas or shorebirds. You won't find beach vendors or hagglers on these shores; just a few tourists and locals enjoying snorkeling or swimming in the gentle surf. High rises are forbidden, with resorts built no taller than three stories.

Fun In The Sun

For most visitors, the real attraction of Provo is the luxury of being able to do nothing at all. Days are spent on the beach or in crystal-clear water. This is considered one of the top scuba destinations in the world. Visibility averages 80 to 100 feet or more and the water temperature is in the low 80s in summer and the mid-70s in winter. Beneath the calm waves swim colorful marine animals as exotic as hawksbill turtles, nurse sharks and octopus. With a one-mile vertical coral wall located offshore, Provo is a diver's paradise; Grand Turk offers miles of drop-off diving; and South Caicos provides many ledge and wall dives. Wreck divers can explore the **HMS Endymion**, which went down in a storm in 1790, leaving behind cannons and anchors off Salt Cay. One of the more unusual dive sites (also visible from the air) is the **Blue**

Turks & Caicos

Hole, a depression hundreds of feet deep in the reef off Middle Caicos. It's filled with pelagics, including sharks, rays and groupers.

From December through April, ecotourists journey to Salt Cay for a chance to spot humpback whales, watching for the giant mammals from shore or in the water in scuba gear. Ecotravelers can enjoy birdwatching on North Caicos and may spot rock iguanas on **Little Water Cay**. The cay is home of a new nature trail program, one of 33 nature reserves and refuges in the Turks and Caicos. Visitors can watch the iguanas in their natural habitat from raised boardwalks and observation towers. Trips to Little Water Cay are offered by several operators who also schedule full-day excursions to the inhabited but sparsely developed islands of North and Middle Caicos for viewing a pink flamingo colony, talking with local residents and a enjoying a beach barbecue. Monthly "glow worm" cruises are another unique experience for travelers. Scheduled from three to six nights after a full moon, these cruises take visitors to the Caicos Bank for a look at a phosphorescent marine worm that lights the waters about an hour after sunset in a unusual mating ritual.

Ecotravel

To protect the ecology of the islands, the Turks and Caicos have established an extensive national park and nature reserve system. Over 31 national parks dot the islands, including **Provo's Princess Alexandra National Park**, with 13 miles of protected beaches, the **NW Point Marine**, with spectacular wall diving and **Chalk Sound**, with small boat sailing on the west end of the island. National park rules make it illegal to hunt or fish, remove any animal or coral, moor vessels over 60 feet except on fixed buoys or bring boats within 100 yards of the shoreline.

JoJo

One of the most protected treasures in the islands is JoJo the dolphin. This wild dolphin has been sighted for 12 years along the north coast of Provo, the only case ever documented of prolonged interaction between an individual wild dolphin and humans. Often spotted swimming along the north shore or near boats, JoJo is protected and the government has declared him a national treasure.

JoJo is rarely seen, but he does have his own website: www.jojo.pc. The JoJo Project pays for medical costs associated with the dolphin. Memberships are available for $50 from the JoJo Project, PO Box 153, Providenciales, Turks and Caicos, or by calling or faxing ☎ 649/941-5617.

Vacationers are certain to spot other wildlife on daytrips to nearby **Water Cay**. Located northeast of Provo, this small island is the home of numerous iguanas that greet boat passengers and happily pose for photos just yards away. Snorkeling cruises take visitors from Provo to this island most every afternoon.

Travelers' Information

Banking

The Turks and Caicos is fast emerging in the international banking world much like the Cayman Islands. There's no shortage of banking facilities on Provo, options are limited on the smaller islands. Barclays and Bank of Nova Scotia both have branches on Provo. Bank hours are 8:30-12:30 and 2-4:30, Monday through Thursday, and 8-12:30, 2-4:30 on Friday.

Turks & Caicos

Climate

Summer highs average about 90°; winter highs about 75°. The hottest months are August to November. Trade winds drop then, and days can be sultry.

Currency

The US dollar is the official currency of Turks and Caicos.

Customs

Vacationers may bring in one carton of cigars or cigarettes, one bottle of liquor or wine, and perfume for personal use.

Credit Cards

Major credit cards are accepted at most establishments.

Crime

These islands have a low crime rate. However, as in any destination, take commonsense precautions while traveling. Don't leave valuables on the beach while you swim; use hotel safes; and be aware of your surroundings, especially during the evening hours.

Departure Tax

There is a departure tax of $15 per person (not apllicable to those under 12 years of age.

Driving

Driving is British style, on the *left* side of the road. A valid driver's license from home will be needed. There is a vehicle rental tax of $10 for cars and $5 for scooters.

Electricity

Throughout these islands the standard is 120/240 volts/60 cycles.

Entry Requirements

US visitors must show proof of citizenship, such as a birth certificate or voter registration card, as well as photo identification or a passport. Visitors must also show a return ticket.

Health/Hospitals

Grand Turk is home to a 36-bed hospital. Provo has medical clinics as well as a hyperbaric chamber.

Internet site

The official Turks and Caicos Website is at www.turksand caicostourism.com.

Language

English is the official language.

Pets

Incoming pets must have all required shots and a veterinarian's certificate. Check with your local vet for current requirements.

Telephone

Good phone service is available from these islands, but it's very expensive. It is cheaper to have someone call you from home or to send a fax. A phone card is needed to use telephone booths. Cards (in $5, $10 and $15 denominations) may be purchased at the Cable & Wireless offices as well as at island stores.

Time Zone

The islands operate on Eastern Standard Time. From April through October, Daylight Savings Time is observed.

Turks & Caicos

Tipping

Fifteen percent tip is standard for restaurant service.

Tourism Office

For information on the islands, ☎ 800/241-0824 or write Turks & Caicos Tourist Office, 11645 Biscayne Boulevard, Suite 302, North Miami, FL 33181. The local number is ☎ 305/891-4117, fax 305/891-7096. Their on-island address is PO Box 128, Grand Turk, Turks and Caicos Islands, ☎ 649/946-2321, fax 649/946-2733.

Vaccinations

No vaccinations or immunizations are required.

Water

Water is safe to drink throughout the islands.

Shopping

The Turks and Caicos may have a lot of attributes that make them attractive to vacationers, but shopping isn't one of them. You will find limited shops on Provo, most in a complex called **Ports of Call,** designed to resemble an old Caribbean seaside town. Look for restaurants, crafts and art in this new development near Grace Bay.

Conch (pronounced Konk) shells make a wonderful souvenir from these islands. Stop by the **Conch Farm** on Provo to purchase a beautiful shell. You'll also find some large shell piles next to some of the island bars. Here you may stop and make an inexpensive purchase and enjoy a cocktail at the same time.

For Caribbean art, check out the **Bamboo Gallery** on Provo, an excellent facility that's been featured in many newspaper and magazine articles. Here you'll find Haitian, Jamaican and even some Turks and Caicos artwork. Near Ports of Call, **Maison Creole** also has magnificent artwork with crafts from Haiti and other Caribbean islands.

Getting There

❊ Arriving By Air

The Turks and Caicos Islands have three international airports: **Providenciales, Grand Turk** and **South Caicos**. Most visitors arrive in Providenciales. Small domestic airports are found on all the other islands, with the exceptions of East and West Caicos, both uninhabited.

Twice-daily jet service to Providenciales is available on **American Airlines** from Miami. Flying time is approximately 80 minutes. Inter-island scheduled service is available on **Turks and Caicos Airways** (☎ 649-946-4255). Inter-island charters and charters to other Caribbean islands can be booked on **Interisland Airways** (☎ 649-941-5481) or **SkyKing** (☎ 649-941-KING).

Getting Around

❊ Rental Cars

Rental cars are available, but they can be tough to obtain (because of the limited numbers) and expensive – about $45 a day for economy size, $59 for a full-size. Once you have a rental car, you'll find that gasoline prices are equally expensive, running about $2.50 a gallon.

Turks & Caicos

⁙ Travel By Taxi

Taxi service is good, especially on Provo, where you can call the **Paradise Taxi Company** (☎ 13555) or **Provo Taxi Association** (☎ 65481). **Nell's Taxi and Tours** (☎ 13228 or 10051) offers island tours at $25 per hour and dinner transportation for $6 per person, round-trip, to any island restaurant (minimum four persons).

Tastes of the Turks & Caicos

With its arid climate, these islands are not the breadbasket tropical islands of Jamaica or St. Lucia fame. Little is grown here; most items must be imported and grocery prices attest to that.

However, you will find a few items grown locally. North Caicos is home to sea grapes, sugar apples, mangoes and sapodillas. Also, the surrounding seas are rich in seafood, including grouper, tuna, hogfish and shellfish such as conch and spiny lobster. You'll also see turtle, dolphin (the fish, not the mammal) and goat on some area menus. A hydroponic farm on Provo supplies some vegetables.

You'll find a wide selection of food in these islands, reflecting the popular tourism industry as well as the many number of ex-pats who make the Turks and Caicos their home.

Both resort and freestanding restaurants offer visitors a variety of cuisines, from Caribbean offerings to Mexican and Italian dishes. Several restaurants feature gourmet cuisine in an elegant atmosphere, others offer island dining in a super-casual atmosphere.

Drinks of the Turks & Caicos

Caya beer, both Pilsner and pale ale, is available in bottles and draft. These brews are bottled by the Turks and Caicos Brewing Company. The local rum, made from sugar cane grown on other islands, is **Lucayan**. This dark rum is distilled by the Lucayan Rum Company Limited.

Purple Gecko Cocktail, Gecko Grille, Ocean Club

☀ Famous for the award-winning Gecko Grille dining room, it is no surprise that this seaside resort serves a prize-worthy cocktail. How to capture a Purple Gecko:

- *1½ ounces tequila*
- *½ ounce blue curaçao*
- *½ ounce red curaçao*
- *1 ounce cranberry juice*
- *1 ounce sour mix*
- *½ ounce lime juice*

Taming the Gecko: Shake all ingredients with ice and pour into a salt-rimmed cocktail glass. Garnish with a lime wedge. ☀

■ ■

Turks & Caicos

Regional Delights

Choosing A Destination

The Turks and Caicos are more than one vacation destination. So where should you go? You will probably be arriving in **Providenciales**, the home of the international airport. This island is the home base for most travelers and attracts scuba divers, snorkelers, nature lovers and anyone looking to get away from it all. Couples, families and singles will find suitable accommodations on this island. Those looking for quiet seclusion may opt for one of the excellent eco-tourism adventures.

Here's a rundown of the various destinations in the Turks and Caicos:

Providenciales

Population: 6,000
Size: 38 square miles

The top tourist destination in the Turks and Caicos, Provo is home to the largest selection of resorts, restaurants and activities. An excellent destination for scuba divers, anglers and those looking for quiet but with all the amenities of a larger destination.

Grand Turk

Population: 4,300
Size: 6 square miles

The capital of the Turks and Caicos is a destination favored by scuba divers and anglers.

North Caicos

Population: 1,300
Size: 41 square miles

The most lush island in this chain makes a good day trip from Provo or a destination for those looking for peace and quiet.

South Caicos

Population: 1,200
Size: 8 square miles

The capital of the Turks and Caicos fishing industry is a good island getaway with few distractions.

Middle Caicos

Population: 300
Size: 48 square miles

This quiet, cave-pocked island can be seen on a day trip and also offers overnight accommodations. A good destination for sportsfishermen and divers.

Salt Cay

Population: 300
Size: 2½ square miles

The smallest of the Turks and Caicos islands, this was once the capital of the area's sea salt industry. Today it offers a very lavish hotel and smaller accommodations aimed at divers.

East Caicos

Population: uninhabited
Size: 18 square miles

A good day trip from Grand Turk or Provo. Offers secluded beaches, scuba diving and sportfishing.

Pine Cay

Population: private
Size: 800 acres

This private island is home to an environmentally sensitive resort open to guests.

⁝⁙ How Much Will It Cost?

Restaurant Dining

Cost of a Meal Per Person
In US dollars, excluding drinks, service and tip
$$$$ - *over $30*
$$$ - *$21-$30*
$$ - *$10-$20*
$ - *Under $10*

Restaurants at All-Inclusive Resorts

Guests at an all-inclusive resort can dine at the restaurant as part of their package. But what if you're not staying at the resort?

Have no fear. We've included the local telephone number so you can call and ask to purchase a day pass. Most all-inclusives sell both day and evening passes, allowing non-guests to enjoy the resort's hospitality. Everyone comes out a winner. You get to try a new restaurant and the resort gets to introduce a traveler to its offerings.

A Hotel Stay

Here's a price breakdown for standard rooms, based on double occupancy in high season under an EP (room-only) plan.

Turks & Caicos

Cost of Accommodations Per Person

In US dollars

$$$$ -	*over $300*
$$$ -	*$201-$300*
$$ -	*$101-$200*
$ -	*Under $100*

For an all-inclusive, where meals, drinks, tips, transportation, and sometimes even more is included, prices are given per person for adults based on double occupancy.

Providenciales

This island boasts the largest portion of the Turks and Caicos population of 15,000, yet it is still open and unsettled. The island is dotted with scrubby growth, short palms and climbing sea grapes, and chalky limestone roads wind across the flat island, connecting settlements like **Blue Hills** and **The Bight**. But the traveler will soon realize that its desert terrain is just a backdrop to the beaches and clear waters that are the main attractions. Some beaches stretch for miles, dotted with only the footprints of iguanas. You won't find beach vendors on these shores, just a few people enjoying snorkeling or a swim in the gentle surf. Highrises are forbidden, and resorts may be no taller than three stories.

For most visitors, the real attraction of Provo is the luxury of being able to do nothing at all. Days are spent on the beach or in water so clear that it is often cited as one of the top scuba destinations in the world. Beneath the calm waves swim exotic colorful marine animals, such as hawksbill turtles, nurse sharks and octopi. With a one-mile vertical coral wall located offshore, Provo is a diver's paradise.

To protect the ecology of the islands, the Turks and Caicos have established an extensive nature reserve system. Over 31 national parks dot the islands, including Provo's **Princess Alexandra National Park**, with 13 miles of protected beaches, the **NW Point Marine**, with spectacular wall diving, and **Chalk Sound**, with small boat sailing on the west end of the island.

You'll find many cuisines represented on the islands. For a real taste of island food, sample the conch, served as fritters, salad and in sandwiches, as well as grouper, hogfish, soft-shell crab and spiny lobster.

Recommended Restaurants

ANACAONA, $$$
Grace Bay Club
☎ *649/946-5050*
Dress code: dressy
Reservations:
recommended

Save one night for a special dinner at Anacaona, an Indian word that translates into "feather of gold." This open-air restaurant is true gold, a gem of a property that combines European elegance with Caribbean tranquillity. Enjoy an elegant meal beneath a thatched palapa that rests on Roman columns. The food is complemented by an extensive wine list and Cuban cigars.

Anacaona is a special place.
Photo courtesy of Grace Bay Club.

Turks & Caicos

Chef Eric Brunel brings his French training and expertise to diners at Anacaona. After extensive European training, Brunel apprenticed at the Ritz Hotel's Ritz Escoffier culinary school in Paris under culinary talents such as Guy Legay, Christian Constant and Michael Roth. He returned to France for awhile and then moved on to Basel, Switzerland, where he merged new classical cuisine tastes and nuances with his French background. Brunel again joined the Ritz Hotel in Paris before beginning his exploration of island cuisine at the Belmont Trusthouse Forte hotel in Bermuda and later at the Reefs Hotel and the award-winning Romanoff restaurant. (During this time, the restaurant was one of few from around the world selected to recreate the "Dinner of the Three Emperors," a Belle Epoque dinner held in Paris in 1867.) After his work in Bermuda, Brunel moved to Virgin Gorda in the British Virgin Islands and spent three years at Little Dix Bay Hotel. He joined Grace Bay Club in March, 1997.

ANGELA'S DELICATESSEN, $
Ports of Call
☎ *649/946-5023*
Dress code: casual
Reservations: not required

Dine inside in a pub-like atmosphere or outdoors under an umbrella at this deli. It serves sandwiches and light meals, including breakfast

ARIZONA BAR AND GRILL, All-inclusive
Beaches Resort and Spa
☎ 649/946-8000
Dress code: casual
Reservations: not required

The Arizona Bar and Grill, decorated in Southwestern style, is one of the more popular dining options at Beaches. Grilled dishes – chicken fajitas, barbecue ribs and Tex-Mex – are favorite options. During the day they offer burgers made to order.

The Arizona Bar and Grill restaurant.

BANANA BOAT CARIBBEAN GRILL, $$
Turtle Cove
☎ 649/946-5706
Dress code: casual
Reservations: not required

This open-air eatery serves local dishes right at the Turtle Cove Marina. Start off with Caribbean nachos (red, blue and yellow corn chips with three cheeses, jalapeños, guacamole, sour cream and jerk spice), conch fritters or potato

Turks & Caicos

skins. Entrées include Caicos lobster and Chicken in Paradise (grilled chicken, pineapple and mozzarella served with Caicos-spiced mayonnaise).

BAREFOOT CAFE, $
Ports of Call
Dress code: casual
Reservations: not required

On a recent trip to Provo, we stayed at the Comfort Inn and started every morning with breakfast at the nearby Barefoot Café. The specialty is the "eggle bagel," which comes with bacon, cheese and egg. Homemade pastries, egg salad croissants, and The Western (scrambled eggs with tomato and onion on a baguette) are other specialties. Breakfast is served all day.

CAICOS CAFE, $$-$$$
Governor's Road, Grace Bay
☎ *649/946-5278*
Dress code: casual
Reservations: suggested

Dine on fresh seafood grilled just steps away from your table at this outdoor eatery. We enjoyed a dinner of jerk chicken (super hot!) and conch chowder. Steak, lamb and barbecue dishes are also available, along with grouper, duck breast and escargots.

CALICO JACK'S, $-$$
Ports of Call
Dress code: casual
Reservations: not required

Located on the upstairs deck of Ports of Call, this eatery features Caribbean favorites. Start with such appetizers as conch salad, then move on to a Rasta veggie burger, jerk chicken sandwich or jerked grouper with peas and rice and coleslaw. It's all served in a casual atmosphere brightened by red and white tablecloths.

COCO BISTRO, $$-$$$
Grace Bay Road
☎ 649/946-5369
Dress code: casually elegant
Reservations: suggested

This restaurant specializes in Mediterranean dishes and Spanish wines. Outdoor tables are shaded by a coconut grove (a unique sight in Provo), and you may also dine inside. Open for dinner only.

DORA'S RESTAURANT AND BAR, $-$$
Leeward Highway
☎ 649/946-4558
Dress code: casual
Reservations: not required

Local dishes are the specialty at this breakfast, lunch and dinner eatery. On Monday and Thursday nights you can enjoy a seafood buffet; live music on Saturday nights brings in many late-night guests.

FAIRWAYS BAR AND GRILL, $$
Provo Golf Course
☎ 649/946-5991
Dress code: golf wear
Reservations: not required

Breakfast and lunch are served at Fairways, as well as dinner on Tuesday through Staurday. As its name suggests, this West Indies-style clubhouse overlooks the greens at Provo Golf Course. It serves sandwiches, salads, fish dishes and more, all acompanied by an extensive selection of Caribbean drinks.

GECKO GRILLE, $$-$$$
Ocean Club
☎ 649/946-5880
Dress code: casually elegant
Reservations: suggested

Start with a drink at the bar then choose and indoor or outdoor table. We always dine outside beneath the ficus trees, lit with small, white Christmas lights. The Gecko Grille is one of our favorite dining spots in these islands, thanks to the creations of Chef John A. Brubaker. "Guests are raving about the Gecko Grille," says Tom Lewis, General Manager. "With over 30 restaurants on the island, we are getting quite agreeable attention not only from Ocean Club guests, but from guests of other resorts and local residents. I believe our success lies in our inventive approach. We believe the rules were made to be broken. We prefer to entertain and please our guests with affordable and imaginative creations rather than just feed the hungry. The proof is in our Shredded Island Pork Pizza, so to speak – visitors say they feel like they've discovered the culinary pulse point of the island after their first meal at Gecko Grille."

Especially impressive at the Gecko Grille is its extensive wine and champagne list. Favorite champagnes include Mumm Cordon Rouge and Moët & Chandon Dom Perignon. Chardonnay choices range from Pine Ridge Knollside Cuvée to Chimney Rock to De Loach from California or Lindeman's Bin 65 from Australia. White burgundy options include a 1993 Corton Charlemagne, a 1994 Puligny Montrachet, and a 1994 Pouilly-Fuisse – all from Josephe Drouhin. Various Bordeaux, merlots and zinfandels round out the list.

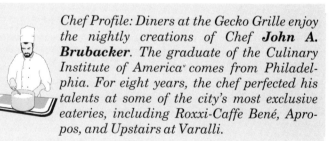

*Chef Profile: Diners at the Gecko Grille enjoy the nightly creations of Chef **John A. Brubacker**. The graduate of the Culinary Institute of America comes from Philadelphia. For eight years, the chef perfected his talents at some of the city's most exclusive eateries, including Roxxi-Caffe Bené, Apropos, and Upstairs at Varalli.*

Sample Dinner Menu, Ocean Club

☀ STARTERS: Spicy conch chowder, a traditional island recipe served in a homemade bread bowl; Provo almond-cracked conch accompanied by Key lime tartar sauce; "ocean escargots," tender young conch served in a garlicky herb butter; jerk shrimp on mango slaw with cilantro and lime; baked Provolone cheese with fire-roasted peppers and brick-oven bread; conch fritters and Brenda's secret sauce; fire-roasted peppers in baked Provolone cheese.

☀ SOUPS AND SALADS: Caesar salad; mixed greens; blackened wahoo or chicken salad served over your choice of mixed greens or Caesar salad; medley of flame-roasted peppers with smoked mozzarella. All salads include your choice of balsamic vinaigrette, almond-citrus dressing or creamy blue cheese dressing. The red conch chowder comes in a sourdough bowl.

☀ BRICK OVEN PIZZA: Traditional cheese pizza comes with your choice of toppings: green peppers, jalapeños, mushrooms, olives, onions, pineapple, bacon, chicken, ground beef, ham, pepperoni, anchovies, conch, grouper and shrimp.

☀ FROM THE GRILLE: Grouper macadamia, encrusted with avocado and macadamia nuts then served over pineapple-tomato salsa; rib-eye steak blackened with Cajun spices or grilled; papaya pork chop marinated in papaya juice and topped with a grilled banana and papaya chutney; grilled chicken breast marinated in papaya juice and topped with a black bean and melon salsa.

☀ PASTA: Linguine Classico, served with a basil-tomato sauce; angel hair tossed with pesto and topped with shrimp and sundried tomatoes; fettucini carbonara; fusilli aglio e olio. All pasta dishes are served with freshly baked garlic bread.

☀ KIDS' MENU: Little Islander burger with French fries; spaghetti served with garlic bread; grilled chicken fingers with honey-mustard sauce and French fries.

☀ DESSERTS: Homemade ice cream served with rich chocolate sauce and banana-nut bread; tiramisu; chocolate mousse cake; Brigitte's apple crisp, an apple raisin delight!

Turks & Caicos

GILLEY'S CAFE AT THE AIRPORT, $-$$
Airport
☎ 649/946-4472
Dress code: casual
Reservations: not required

Didn't have the chance to dine at Gilley's Café at Leeward (below)? You can still grab a taste of local dishes at this snack bar at the airport departure lounge. There is nothing fancy as far as the atmosphere (it's a snack bar), but the food is great.

GILLEY'S CAFE AT LEEWARD, $$
☎ 649/946-5094
Dress code: casual
Reservations: optional

This delightful eatery, located just steps from the marina at Leeward, serves breakfast, lunch and dinner. We dined here on cracked conch, fried to tender perfection; other options include lobster salad, sirloin steak, seafood and broccoli quiche, and more. The simple restaurant offers indoor seating, with long tables that encircle a central bar.

HEY JOSE'S CARIBBEAN CANTINA, $$-$$$
Central Square on Leeward Highway
☎ 649/946-4812
Dress code: casual
Reservations: optional

José's offers a variety of cuisines, including Mexican, Italian pizza and American. The mood here is fun and friendly, with a jukebox and very popular happy hours.

KIMONO, All-inclusive
Beaches Resort And Spa
☎ 649/946-8000
Dress code: casually elegant
Reservations: required

Chefs at Kimono prepare dishes right at your table teppanyaki-style at this fun eatery. Start with Caribbean-style sushi or sweet and sour chicken wings. Be sure to save room for main dishes that include pepper-sherry shrimp, glazed mahi mahi teriyaki and sesame chicken breast.

LE JARDIN RESTAURANT, $$
Le Deck Hotel and Beach Club
Grace Bay
☎ 649/946-5547
Dress code: casual
Reservations: optional

This beachside restaurant serves French and European cuisine as well as local favorites such as blackened grouper, fish and chips and cracked conch. Live music entertains diners and a late-night crowd on Thursdays and Sundays (also the day for the weekly buffet). The open-air eatery is fun and casual. A favorite with locals.

LONE STAR BAR AND GRILL, $-$$
Ports of Call
☎ 649/946-5832
Dress Code: casual
Reservations: not required

Located at Ports of Call shopping center, this upstairs restaurant specializes in Tex-Mex fare such as fajitas and tacos. It has a casual bar atmosphere. Live music on Friday nights brings in a crowd. You'll find locals and vacationers alike in this lively spot.

MARCO POLO'S RESTAURANT, $$
Ports of Call
☎ 649/946-5129
Dress code: casual
Reservations: not required

This second-floor restaurant located in Ports of Call shopping center featrues Italian dishes on "Marco Polo's Great Voyage" menu. Enjoy fettucine alfredo, spaghetti with meatballs or veal parmigana. We visited here on a Friday night and found the atmosphere lively and fun, with diners enjoying dinner in the small diner and then stepping out on the balcony to listen to live music next door.

Turks & Caicos

Ports of Call shopping center.

SAPODILLA'S, All-inclusive
Beaches Resort and Spa
☎ *649/946-8000*
Dress code: dressy
Reservations: required

International cuisine served in a luxurious atmosphere brings diners to this eatery. Specialties include cânapés Beaches, a puff pastry shell filled with mushrooms, apples, onions and bacon splashed with curry cream sauce; fillet of red snapper; filet mignon; and blackened pork tenderloin.

SCHOONER'S, All-inclusive
Beaches Resort and Spa
☎ *649/946-8000*
Dress code: dressy
Reservations: required

Schooner's serves up local and imported seafood with a gourmet flair. Start with steamed mussels in white wine sauce or conch salad, then move on to grilled snapper with peppercorn sauce, pan-fried salmon, Alaskan king crab legs, surf and turf or grilled lobster tails.

SHARKBITE BAR AND GRILL, $$
Admiral's Club at Turtle Cove
☎ 649-941-5090
Dress code: casual
Reservations: not required

This waterfront dining option serves lunch and dinner daily. It is Provo's only sports bar, offering a nightly happy hour with free food. The menu lists American and local offerings, including fish and chips.

SUNSET BAR AND GRILL, $$
Erebus Inn
☎ 649/941-5445 or 946-4240
Dress: casually elegant
Reservations: suggested

Fine dining with a French flair is the specialty at this indoor and outdoor restaurant. Open for breakfast, lunch and dinner. With its French ownership, the Sunset Bar and Grill provides a taste of the island, Gallic style.

THE TERRACE RESTAURANT, $$-$$$
Turtle Cove Inn
☎ 649/946-4763
Dress code: casual
Reservations: suggested

We have fond memories of dining outdoors at this upstairs restaurant. Specialties are conch and local seafood, always prepared with a creative twist. Open for lunch and dinner daily except Sunday. Service here is fast and friendly. Many diners are locals, and there are a lot of repeat visitors from out of town too.

TIKI HUT, $
Turtle Cove Inn
☎ 649/941-5341
Dress code: casual
Reservations: not required

This casual restaurant starts the day with Grand Marnier croissants, French toast, Belgian waffles and tropical pancakes... and it gets better from there. We enjoyed

Turks & Caicos

an excellent lunch here and sampled the conch fritters, made from the Conch Farm's own product; fish and chips; and jerk chicken sandwich. Other options include pizza, pasta and fish combos and Colorado Black Angus beef. An excellent cellar offers a selection of wines from around the world. Open for breakfast, lunch and dinner daily. Box lunches can be prepared for you to tote with you on your day's outing.

The restaurant is located at the marina and has a fun, boat-loving atmosphere with many locals and ex-pat diners as well as vacationers.

Sample Dinner Menu, Tiki Hut

❖ PASTA: Caicos lobster in a spicy marinara and cream sauce served over fresh fettucine; King salmon sautéed in a lemon-dill champagne cream sauce; four-cheese lasagna, with mozzarella, ricotta, cheddar and parmesan; ziti in marinara sauce topped with mozzarella and baked; fettucini fruits of the sea – clams, shrimp, lobster, conch and fresh fish sautéed in a white wine, garlic and herb cream sauce served over fresh egg fettucine; rigatoni carbonara; linguine primavera; fettuccine Alfredo.

❖ PIZZA: The Sicilian (grilled chicken, prosciutto and basil); The North American (pepperoni, green pepper, mushroom); The Cajun Zoo (langostino tails, shrimp and Cajun spices); The Turks Islander (lobster and diced conch); The Rajun' Cajun (chicken, sautéed onion and spices); The BBQ Chicken (BBQ sauce, BBQ chicken, onion and green pepper); The Basilica (pesto, black olives, feta cheese and sundried tomatoes); The Veggie (onion, pepper, tomato, mushroom and olives); The Great Divide (ground beef, mushrooms and onions); The South Pacific (ham, pineapple, mango and crushed red pepper); The Plain Jane (just cheese and more cheese).

❖ FRESH FISH. These fresh catches are available grilled, jerked or blacked and are served with Caesar or garden salad and sautéed vegetables: mahi-mahi, Caicos grouper; Caicos red snapper; yellowfin tuna; swordfish; halibut; wahoo (in season); lobster tail (in season).

Where To Stay

☀ The Turks and Caicos Islands currently offers a total of 1,500 guest rooms, most found on Providenciales. Accommodations range from full-service resorts to small properties and guesthouses.

ALLEGRO RESORT TURKS AND CAICOS, $$
Grace Bay
☎ *800/858-2258*
www.allegroresorts.com

☀ The Allegro Resort is the former Turquoise Reef Resort, always a favorite accommodation on Provo and well known for its great beach and extensive watersports. After a $22.5-million renovation with its purchase by Allegro Resorts, the property opened as an all-inclusive, complete with a supervised childrens' program.

BEACHES TURKS AND CAICOS, $$
☎ *800/BEACHES, 649/946-8000, fax 649/946-8001*
www.beaches.com

☀ Part of the Sandals chain, this all-inclusive is a favorite with families. The 224-room resort, set on the 12-mile beach at Grace Bay, is open to singles, couples and families.

There are several dining options. Reflections, the main dining room, features a buffet for breakfast, lunch and dinner. Sapodilla's and Schooner's serve adults only, while families are welcome in the Arizona Bar and Grill for Tex-Mex cuisine or at the Teppanyaki restaurant, Kimonos. A nursery is available for infants and toddlers, while the Cuda Kids Club keeps older children happy at the children's pool, kids gazebo, playground, table tennis area and pool table facilities. The club offers classes in everything from sandcastle building to reggae. Video game buffs will love the Sega Center with state-of-the-art video games (all complimentary). Teens also have special activities, including disco nights, movie nights, sports tournaments and more.

Turks & Caicos

Guest facilities include a dive shop, fitness center, spa, tennis and meeting facilities for up to 185 attendees.

CLUB MED-TURKOISE, $$
Grace Bay Beach. All-inclusive
☎ *800/258-2633, 649/946-5500, fax 649/946-5501*
www.clubmed.com

Along with Beaches, Club Med is the most action-packed place to stay and is popular with singles and couples. It has welcomed guests for over 15 years. It has 298 rooms, a dive center (extra charge) and other watersports, as well as tennis, fitness center and a nightclub. Other fun: circus workshops, deep-sea fishing, sailing, soccer, softball, volleyball – the list goes on. Guests must be 18 years or over. There are three restaurants; non-guests may purchase day and night passes.

Club Med's Mai Tai in a Pineapple

- *3 ounces light rum*
- *½ ounce lime juice*
- *¼ teaspoon triple sec*
- *¼ teaspoon orzata*
- *½ teaspoon sugar*

Garnish
- *1 slice lime*
- *1 sprig mint*

Mix liquids. Serve in hollow pineapple. *Serves one.* ☀

Club Med's Planter's Punch in Orange

- *1½ ounces dark rum*
- *3 ounces orange juice*
- *½ ounce lemon juice*
- *1 teaspoon sugar*
- *¼ teaspoon grenadine*

Garnish
- *½ slice orange*
- *1 slice of lemon*

Mix liquids, add garnish. *Serves one.* ☀

COMFORT SUITES, $
Grace Bay
☎ 800/992-2015

The latest addition to the lodging scene is this Comfort Suites, adjacent to Ports of Call shopping center. The 99-room property offers rooms with one king-size bed or two double beds; rooms include a sofabed and small refrigerator as well. There is no restaurant on site, although a complimentary continental breakfast is served daily and several restaurants are located at Ports of Call.

EREBUS INN, $$
Turtle Cove
☎ 800/645-1179, 649/946-4240, fax 649/946-4704

Overlooking Turtle Cove Marina, this modest inn is a charming spot for those on a budget – plus it offers a great view. Amenities include a gym and a freshwater pool as well as an excellent restaurant on the property (see page 183).

GRACE BAY CLUB, $$$$
Grace Bay
☎ 800/946-5050 or 869/946-5757, fax 649/946-5758
www.gracebayclub.com

Provo's most exclusive property is this Swiss-owned hotel with a high regard for privacy. Furnished with items from Mexico and India, the rooms are decorated in subdued beige tones to emphasize on the brilliant color of the sea just beyond the balcony.

Outside, the Grace Bay Club also exudes an elegant look. The Spanish-style buildings, with their terra-cotta tiled roofs and stone columns, contrast to the blue sea and the brilliant tropical hibiscus and bougainvillea. Guests enjoy many watersports here, from quiet Sunfish sails to snorkeling in the pristine waters. Scuba diving, bonefishing, sea kayaking and sailing excursions can be arranged.

Turks & Caicos

Beautiful Grace Bay Club.

Guest accommodations include 21 guest suites with private balconies on the oceanfront. All have cable television, air-conditioning, in-room safes, fax machines (upon request), ceiling fans, kitchen facilities with refrigerator and ice maker, washer and dryer, twice-daily maid service, room service, marble baths and hair dryer. Recreational options include tennis, watersports and bicycling. The resort is also home to the gourmet Anacaona restaurant, which uses only natural ingredients and local seafood.

LE DECK, $$
Grace Bay
☎ *800/528-1905, 649/946-5547, fax 649/946-5770*

Le Deck has comfortable recently refurbished rooms, an excellent restaurant and a central location. Nothing fancy, but you can't beat the Grace Bay location. The beachfront property includes a freshwater swimming pool.

OCEAN CLUB, $$
Grace Bay
☎ *800/457-8787, 649/946-5880, fax 649/946-5845*

Starting as a simple timeshare, the property has grown to full resort status with a small shopping arcade, convenience store, watersports concession, restaurant, beach grill and two bars. The all-suite Grace Bay property still functions as a timeshare, but now takes its place alongside other full-service resorts on a 12-mile stretch of beach.

Expansive rooms greet even those guests who choose the smaller accommodations at Ocean Club. With white tile floors, wicker furnishings, sliding glass doors opening to screened patios and balconies, and numerous windows, suites here are sunny and styled in a casual beachfront decor. Every room has air-conditioning, fully equipped kitchens or kitchenettes, cable TV, direct dial phones with voice messaging, in-suite washer and dryer and daily maid service. Families will appreciate the rollaway beds and baby cribs; high chairs are available. Two children under 12 may stay with parents at no cost in the same suite.

The pool at Ocean Club.

The resort's white sand beach is one of Ocean Club's top assets, located just steps from the suites. Water lovers can also choose from two freshwater pools, including a freeform pool that's a favorite with young vacationers. Art Pickering's Provo Turtle Divers is situated at the resort, offering dive excursions and watersports, including snorkeling, bonefishing and deep-sea fishing, parasailing and scuba certification.

The fitness center has stationary bikes, a Universal station, Stairclimbers and free weights, and also offers massages and aromatherapy, which also may be enjoyed in-room. Tennis is available day and night on a lighted court. There's also a nearby golf course.

A dining shuttle operates nightly for drop-offs at island restaurants; a shopping shuttle runs three days a week, primarily to the island supermarket so guests can stock their kitchens. The front desk staff arranges for rental cars, scooters, bicycles and babysitters, as well as island tours and day sails aboard private sailing charters such as the *Beluga*, a 37-foot catamaran.

Ocean Club has 83 units with full kitchens, screened balconies and porches. Guests may dine at the Gecko Grill restaurant, which features a Culinary Institute of America-trained chef.

Currently, Ocean Club is adding Ocean Club West, located next to Grace Bay Club. The new facilities will start with 30 guest units.

Grouper Macadamia, Gecko Grille

- *2 pounds fresh grouper filet, cut into 4-ounce portions*
- *2 tablespoons butter*
- *1 tablespoon salt*
- *1 tablespoon pepper*
- *1 avocado, peeled, seeded and puréed*
- *1 lime, juiced*
- *½ cup macadamia nuts, toasted and rough chopped*
- *1 cup pineapple-tomato salsa*

Garnish:

- *4 lemon wedges*
- *4 lime wedges*
- *8 sprigs fresh cilantro*

Grease a baking pan with butter. Place grouper onto pan and season with salt and pepper. Place in oven and bake at 350°F for five to 10 minutes (until fish is almost cooked). Remove from oven. Place avocado flesh and lime juice in blender and purée. Spread avocado-lime purée on top of fish and sprinkle with macadamia nuts. Place back into oven until fish is cooked and macadamia nuts are hot. Place a dollop of the pineapple-tomato salsa on the center of a plate.

Arrange two pieces of grouper on either side of the salsa. Garnish with lemon and lime wedges. Top with two sprigs of the fresh cilantro. *Yields four servings.* ☀

Pineapple-Tomato Salsa, Gecko Grille

- *2 cups pineapple, cored and diced*
- *10 plum tomatoes, peeled, seeded and diced*
- *¼ cup green pepper, diced*
- *¼ cup scallion, thin sliced*
- *¼ cup yellow onion, diced*
- *6 garlic cloves, chopped*
- *1-2 jalapeño peppers, fine chopped*
- *1 bunch fresh cilantro, chopped*
- *¼ cup white vinegar*
- *½ cup olive oil*
- *1 tablespoon salt*
- *1 tablespoon black pepper*

Combine all ingredients in a bowl and mix until blended. Adjust seasoning with salt and pepper. Transfer to a storage container and refrigerate until ready to use. ☀

■ ■

TURTLE COVE INN, $
Turtle Cove
☎ *800/887-0477, 649/946-4203, fax 649/946-4141*

When divers come up for air, many stay at this resort, which offers special dive packages through its on-site dive center. The inn is located directly off the marina. Rooms are simple but include telephone, cable TV and a private balcony. A freshwater pool is available for guests, along with a casual restaurant and bar.

Between Meals

Conch Farm
☎ *649/946-5849*
Hours: 9 - 4, Monday - Saturday
Admission: fee
This is the only farm in the world that raises queen conch, the shellfish that's become a favorite treat throughout much of the Caribbean. On a guided tour, you'll see conch in various stages, from the larvae in the hatchery to juveniles about four millimeters in length, right up to adulthood. The operation has three million conch in inventory. There is a gift shop. The product of this unique farm is served at area restaurants, including the Gecko Grille, Anacaona restaurant and the Tiki Hut.

Queen conch.

Little Water Cay
Admission: free

Save a day to cruise over to Little Water Cay, an island inhabited by friendly iguanas and tropical birds. Most watersports operators on Provo bring day trippers out to this island just off the east end of Provo. The cay is home to the new Little Water Cay Nature Trail, designed so that the 20,000 visitors who come to this small island every year can enjoy but not disturb the 1,500 to 2,000 endangered West Indian rock iguanas. Boardwalks have been constructed to allow visitors to see the iguanas and their burrowing systems. You can also climb into observation towers for a view of the cay and the waters.

An iguana sunning at Little Water Cay.

Turks & Caicos

Working Off Those Meals

⁑ Golf

Provo Golf Club.

Vacationers looking for the opportunity to golf will find it at the 18-hole championship **Provo Golf Club** (☎ 649/946- 5991, fax 649/946-5992), frequently cited as one of the top 10 courses in the Caribbean. The club has a pro shop and the Fairways Bar and Grill, which serves breakfast or lunch. You can hone your skills at a driving range or on putting greens. Eighteen holes, including a shared cart, is $95 ($60 for nine holes); a three-round package is available for $250. Clubs may be rented ($18 for 18 holes; $12 for nine holes). Golf packages are available from most Provo hotels.

⁑ Scuba Diving

Scuba diving and snorkeling are the top attractions in these islands. Visibility ranges from 80 to 100 feet or better and water temperatures hover at about 82° in the summer and 75 or so in the winter months. Beneath the calm waves swim colorful marine animals as exotic as hawksbill turtles, nurse sharks and octopus. With a one-mile vertical coral wall located offshore, Provo is a diver's paradise.

Top dive operators are ready to help you get under the waves.

Art Pickering's Provo Turtle Divers, Turtle Cove Marina, ☎ 649/946-4232.

Caicos Adventures, Banana Cabana at Turtle Cove Marina, ☎ 649/941-3346.

Flamingo Divers, Turtle Cove Landing, ☎ 649/946-4193.

Le Deck Diving Centre, Le Deck Hotel, Grace Bay, ☎ 649/946-5547.

Ocean Outback, Grace Bay, ☎ 649/941-5810 or 946-4393.

Sea Dancer, Caicos Marina & Shipyard, 305/669-9391.

Silver Deep - Provo Wall Divers, Blue Hills, ☎ 649/941-5595.

Turks & Caicos Aggressor, Liveaboard dive boat, 504/385-2416.

Turtle Inn Divers, ☎ 649/942-3346.

Grand Turk

☀ Grand Turk is home of its own little historic controversy. Remember we said earlier in the book that many historians believe Columbus first made landfall in the New World on the Bahamian island of San Salvador? Well, many others believe that the island the Italian explorer called "Guanahani" wasn't the Bahamian island, but instead was Grand Turk.

Beachside homes in Turks & Caicos.

The truth about where Columbus first set foot on land may never be known, but many facts are proven about Grand Turk's often raucous history. The island was settled by pirates from Bermuda.

Pirate Haven

These devilish entrepreneurs used the nearby coral reefs as their own traps, luring ships in with lights to a false sense of safety. When the ships wrecked on the coral reefs, out went the pirates to plunder the vessels. Today, evidence of that wicked history is still apparent on Grand Turk; many of the historic buildings were built from the lumber of these ships.

The atmosphere is quiet and calm on Grand Turk. This island serves as the governmental capital of the Turks and Caicos Islands and you'll see many government buildings in the community of **Cockburn Town**, where most of the island's 4,300 residents live just steps from the sea.

The waterfront at Grand Turk.

Recommended Restaurants

ARAWAK INN RESTAURANT AND BAR, $-$$
*2 miles south of Cockburn Town. Follow Waterloo Road to
Harbor Sands area at end of island.*
☎ *649/946-2277 or 2276*
Dress code: casual
Reservations: not required

☀ You can enjoy local as well as American dishes at this casual eatery, and seafood is the specialty of the house. On Saturday nights they offer a barbecue. Other nights, you can dine indoors or outside with a view of the sea. Open for breakfast, lunch and dinner.

SECRET GARDEN, $$
Salt Raker Inn, Duke Street
☎ 649/946-2260
Dress code: casual
Reservations: not required

The restaurant is open for breakfast, lunch and dinner and features local cuisine as well as American dishes. On Wednesday and Sunday nights it hosts a barbecue and sing-a-long. The atmosphere here is friendly and fun. This a good spot to swap scuba diving adventures.

TURKS HEAD INN, $-$$
☎ 946/649-2466
Duke Street
Dress code: casually elegant
Reservations: not required

This casual eatery serves breakfast, lunch and dinner. Start the evening in the pub or stop by for an after-dinner drink and local music. Caribbean cuisine is the house specialty, served along with a selection of wines.

THE WATER'S EDGE, $-$$
Duke Street
☎ 946/649-1680
Dress code: casual
Reservations: not required

This bistro offers local seafood dishes in a fun and relaxing setting on the beach. Lunch and dinner.

Where To Stay

ARAWAK INN AND BEACH CLUB, $$
White Sands Beach, on the southwest side of the island
☎ 888/880-4477, 649-946-2277, fax 649-946-2279
E-mail: reservations@arawakinn.com
www.arawakinn.com

This hotel sits to the south of Governor's Beach. It offers 15 units. Diving and horseback riding are available.

CORAL REEF CONDOMINIUMS
AND BEACH CLUB, $
The Ridge
☎ *800/418-4704, 649/946-2055, fax 649/946-2911*
E-mail: gthotels@tciway.tc

Located on the island's windward side, Coral Reef provides 18 studio and one-bedroom apartment units with kitchen facilities, telephones and cable TV. Guests have access to the freshwater swimming pool, Jacuzzi, tennis, fitness center and meeting facilities.

SALT RAKER INN, $-$$
Duke Street
☎ *649/946-2260, fax 649/946-2817*
E-mail sraker@tciway.tc
www.microplan.com/~paradise

This small property has just 10 guest rooms and three suites, each with air-conditioning, cable TV and ceiling fans. The inn is home to The Secret Garden restaurant and is within walking distance to the beach.

SITTING PRETTY HOTEL, $$
Cockburn Town
☎ *800/418-4704, 649/946-2232, fax 649/946-2668*

Formerly the Hotel Kittina, Sitting Pretty includes a 5-star PADI dive shop alongside its 24 air-conditioned guest rooms. Some of the rooms are situated right on the beach in Cockburn Town; others are across the street. There's a pool, restaurant and bar.

TURKS HEAD INN, $-$$
Duke Street
☎ *649/946-2466, fax 649/0946-2825*

This circa 1860 mansion was once a governor's private guest house and now offers antique-filled air-conditioned guest rooms, a restaurant, bar and live entertainment some evenings.

Turks & Caicos

Between Meals

Turks and Caicos National Museum
Main Street, Cockburn Town
☎ *649/946-2160*
Hours: Monday through Friday, 10-4, Saturday, 10-1
Admission: fee
It may have been, as the story always goes, a dark and stormy night that caused the Molasses Reef shipwreck nearly 500 years ago. Or the weather may have been perfectly clear, the ship lured onto the coral by buccaneers on the shore falsely signaling safe passage.

Whatever the reason, the Spanish caravel hit the reef in the Turks and Caicos Islands, sinking quickly in only 20 feet of water. There it remained, encased in a heavy coat of sediment and barnacles, until the 1970s. When the wreck was excavated, it proved to be the oldest European shipwreck in the New World.

Today, artifacts from the vessel are on display in the Turks and Caicos National Museum, itself a buried treasure. The museum is a quick hop by commuter airplane from Providenciales. With interactive displays, video presentations and scientific exhibits, this would be a special attraction in any city with a rich maritime history, but it is especially surprising, however, to find it on an island only seven miles square with a population of only 3,700.

The museum is located in the former Guinip House, one of the oldest buildings on Grand Turk. The 150-year-old home was built in the Colonial style used by the Bermudans who settled this island. Like many other Grand Turk buildings, the house was constructed from the lumber of wrecked wooden ships.

The attention of the world was focused on the Turks and Caicos during the excavation of this wreck when the initial salvagers tried to claim that this was Columbus' *Pinta*. In reality, the ship was not a part of Columbus' fleet, but one whose purpose was probably illegal. "We don't know the name of this ship," explains curator Brian M. Riggs, "but we know why we don't know."

Like drug-running planes of today, ships transporting illegal booty were purposely kept off the official records of Spain. Three pair of two-person leg irons, recovered in a locked position, and rare Lucayan pottery indicate that the ship was probably en route with illegal slaves, bound for the plantations of Hispaniola.

Salvagers were trying to obtain funding by claiming this was the *Pinta*, but the government of the Turks and Caicos reclaimed the wreck and turned it over to the Texas A&M-based Ships of Discovery, a nonprofit archaeological research group. The group took over the laborious task of removing items and carefully cataloging each piece, then trying to undo the years of damage the sea had wrought.

Today, many of those artifacts can be seen in this museum. Three downstairs rooms are dedicated to shipwrecks, with one room covering the Molasses Reef site, another the archaeology and scientific processes involved in an excavation, and the third filled with artifacts. Other exhibits explain more about the structure of Age of Discovery caravel ships and the history of the Turks and Caicos.

Working Off Those Meals

☵ Scuba Diving

The waters which for so many years sheltered shipwrecks are a favorite with scuba divers. Grand Turk has miles of drop-off diving surrounding its shores. Night dives are especially popular, when the reefs take on a phosphorescent glow.

In Grand Turk, check with **Blue Water Divers**, ☎ 649/946-2432; **Sea Eye Diving**, ☎ 649/946-1407; and **Aquanaut**, ☎ 649/946-2160.

North Caicos

☼ They call it the "Garden Island," and a quick look around North Caicos explains why. This island receives twice as much rain as Providenciales and most other destinations in the Turks and Caicos. The rainfall helps it produce most of the fruit which comes from these isles: sea grapes, sugar apples, oranges, mangoes and other tropical harvests.

This island is home to the ruins of several Loyalists **plantations**. Another interesting site is the **Flamingo Pond**, where magnificent flamingos nest. These birds can also be sighted at the **Mud Hold Pond**. Birders should make time to visit nearby **Three Mary's Cay** for a look at ospreys.

Recommended Restaurants

OCEAN BEACH HOTEL RESTAURANT, $$
Whitby
☎ *649/946-7113*
Dress code: casual, casually elegant
Reservations: required

☼ This restaurant, located at Ocean Beach Condominiums, serves lunch and dinner by reservation only. Dine on Caribbean or international dishes at this popular restaurant that's favored by locals and visitors alike.

PROSPECT OF WHITBY
HOTEL RESTAURANT, $$-$$$
Whitby
☎ *649/946-7119*
Dress code: casually elegant
Reservations: recommended

Feast on Italian cuisine at this restaurant that is open for breakfast, lunch and dinner.

PELICAN BEACH HOTEL RESTAURANT, $$
Whitby
☎ *649/946-7112*
Dress code: casual
Reservations: suggested

Dine indoors or out at this hotel restaurant that features local and American dishes. Local dishes include fresh fish and Caribbean lobster, as well as native conch. They also serve chicken and ribs.

Where To Stay

OCEAN BEACH HOTEL/CONDO, $-$$$
Whitby
☎ *649/946-7113, fax 649/946-7386*

This seven-room hotel offers snorkeling and scuba diving. All rooms are on the oceanfront and include a private bath, ceiling fan, rattan furniture and a sliding glass door to the outside. You'll also find a pool and a tour desk that offers bike and car rentals and excursions. It also has a restaurant.

Turks & Caicos

PELICAN BEACH HOTEL, $$-$$$
Whitby
☎ *649/946-7112, fax 649/946-7139*

This 14-room hotel offers boat rentals, scuba diving and tennis. Travelers enjoy watersports and can also explore local caves, plantation house ruins or watch pink flamingos at their roost. Each room has a full bath, dressing area, ceiling fans and a terrace.

PROSPECT OF WHITBY HOTEL, $-$$
Whitby
☎ *649/946-7119, fax 649/946-7114*

This relaxed oceanfront resort has 28 guest rooms and features tennis, watersports and fishing. There's also a restaurant. Rooms here are basic, with no distractions to keep you from relaxing – that means no TV, no radio and no daily paper!

Middle Caicos

This middle child is no shy violet; Middle Caicos is larger than its nearby sister islands and sometimes even termed "Grand Caicos." Fifteen miles long and 13 miles wide, the island is largely undeveloped and is home to just 300 residents.

The island has a rich history. The Taíno Indians lived here around 750 AD (they were later renamed the Lucayans when explorers reached the island on the feast of St. Luke's Day). Up to 4,000 Taínos inhabited the island and their artifacts are still being discovered on the sandy beaches and in limestone caves. One archaeological excavation revealed a ceremonial court that also served as a ball court.

Later the island became a pirate's lair. Pierre Le Grande captured a Spanish treasure ship near the islands around 1640, and for years the island served as a hideout for pirates such as Calico Jack Rackam, Ann Bonny and Mary Reade.

The Caves

One aspect of the island that may have attracted those pirates were its many caves. Caves over 120,000 years old are known as the most dramatic above-water caverns in the Caribbean. These Conch Bar Caves, a sacred site to the Taínos, have never been fully explored. Local guides take travelers inside to view the giant stalagmite and stalactite formations, as well as underground lakes. The caves are inhabited by four bat species and giant white owls with a wingspan of five feet.

Where To Stay

BLUE HORIZON RESORT ($$)
☎ *649/946-6141, fax 649-946-6139*

☀ This small property offers rental cottages that have a full kitchen and daily maid service. The property includes a dormitory that takes up to 10 guests (sharing two communal bathrooms), as well as an air-conditioned suite. All guests have use of picnic tables, volleyball court and dart boards.

Working Off Those Meals

☷ Scuba Diving

Dive boats ride over from nearby islands to bring scuba buffs to these clear waters. Reefs and wall dives are available. A favorite dive spot just off the Middle Caicos is the **Blue Hole**. Easily visible from the air, this round depression in the reef is hundreds of feet deep and is a favorite with advanced divers. Sharks, rays, groupers and sea turtles frequent the navy-blue waters of this underwater sinkhole. Operators come from nearby islands to enjoy these waters (see each island section for a listing and contact information).

⁂ Sportfishing

Sportfishing boats come from nearby islands to try their luck in these rich waters. (See listings for Providenciales and other islands.)

Pine Cay

Pine Cay is for those who really want to get away from it all. Privately owned, the 800-acre island is dotted with willowy casuarina trees, pretty beaches and a single resort.

Where To Stay & Eat

THE MERIDIAN CLUB, $$$$
Pine Cay
☎ *800-331-9154, fax 649/946-5128*

At this environmentally sensitive all-inclusive resort, guests enjoy a phone-free visit filled with fun activities, including sailing, windsurfing, snorkeling, fishing, tennis, and bicycling. Dine at the resort's Club House Restaurant, where the award-winning chef offers a selection of fresh fish dishes and other healthy meals.

Salt Cay

Tiny Salt Cay is the kind of place you come to for rest and relaxation. There are very few diversions on this small cay – just some fields that were once flooded with sea-water, later to evaporate and be raked of sea salt. In those days, this 2½-square-mile landmass was the world's largest producer of salt. Remnants of old windmills still turn in the gentle trade winds, a reminder of that bygone era.

Today Salt Cay is a great place to pedal around on a bike and not worry about traffic. Beautiful waters surround the cay, inviting snorkelers and scuba divers.

Recommended Restaurants

MT. PLEASANT GUEST HOUSE, $$
Victoria Street
☎ 649/946-6927
Dress code: casual
Reservations: not required

We have fond memories of an excellent lunch at this casual eatery. We flew to Salt Cay for the day and ate at this garden restaurant located behind the bed and breakfast. After, we enjoyed a walk around town as our pilot napped in a hammock in the garden: true island relaxation. This casual restaurant is an excellent place to meet fellow travelers.

Turks & Caicos

Mount Pleasant.

THE WINDMILLS, $$$-$$$$
North Beach Road
☎ *649/946-6962*
Dress code: casually elegant or dressy
Reservations: required

This elegant eatery oofers a selection of local dishes cooked with a gourmet flair. Try Salt Cay lobster.

Where To Stay

MOUNT PLEASANT GUEST HOUSE, $
Victoria Street
☎ *888/332-3133, 649/946-6927*

This simple accommodation option has seven guest rooms plus a dorm room with multiple beds. It's a favorite with scuba divers. All rooms are furnished with antiques and, while they're nothing fancy, they are within walking distance of the beach. A restaurant is located on property.

Windmills Plantation.

WINDMILLS PLANTATION, $$$$
North Beach Road
☎ *800/822-7715, 649/946-6962, fax 649/946-6930*
E-mail: plantation@tciway.tc

☀ It's surprising to find this exclusive eight-room hotel tucked away here. It has furniture imported from Costa Rica, a library with over 1,000 volumes, a Caribbean restaurant, horseback and nature trails – great for a romantic getaway. The most lavish property on Salt Cay, this all-inclusive has eight rooms and four suites, two with private plunge pools.

Between Meals

Whale Watching
Admission: fee
Hours: December through April only
Nature lovers find plenty of activity on this tiny isle. From December though April, humpback whales can be spotted in

Turks & Caicos

the Turks Islands Passage between Salt Cay and Grand Turk.

Working Off Those Meals

❖ Scuba Diving

Scuba divers find good reef diving as well as the wreck of the *HMS Endymion*. Sinking in a storm in 1790, this wreck was discovered by dive operator and Mount Pleasant innkeeper Brian Sheedy. While much of the wreck has been lost to time, the massive cannons still rest on the ocean's floor, along with four giant anchors.

For scuba diving while on Salt Cay, call **Porpoise Divers**, ☎ 649/946-6927.

South Caicos

☀ South Caicos is not an island you want to visit for activities. Don't look for much to keep you entertained – you're going to have to entertain yourself or just enjoy the peace and quiet of this island, home to much of the Turks and Caicos' fishing industry.

Most activity here takes place in **Cockburn Harbour,** from which conch and spiny lobster are exported. Have a look at the bustling harbor, then hire a taxi driver for a tour of the island. One popular stop is the **boiling hole**, a natural blowhole where the sea is forced through gaps in the stone, spraying water and mist in the air. This is a good stop when there is a lot of wave action. Don't forget to bring your camera.

Where To Stay & Eat

CLUB CARIB BEACH RESORT, $$
& THE SUNSET BAR AND RESTAURANT, $$
East Bay
☎ *800/581-2582, 649/946-3444 (resort);*
☎ *649/946-8114 (restaurant)*
Dress code: casual
Reservations: suggested

Club Carib has16 rooms on the beach and 24 on the water; one- , two- , and three-bedroom suites are available. Each of the rooms has air-conditioning and cable TV. When you're ready for some activity, try scuba diving, sailing, windsurfing or any of the numerous other watersports. You can even arrange to go out with local fishermen. The atmosphere here is relaxed and homey, and you'll meet many repeat guests.

This Sunset Restaurant serves local seafood, including lobster and conch, in a casual, family-friendly setting.

Working Off Those Meals

Scuba Diving

Guided dives and equipment are available through **Club Carib Beach & Harbour Resorts**, ☎ 649/946-3360.

Turks & Caicos

ᵀestivals

For dates and additional information about these festivals, contact the Turks & Caicos Tourist Board, ☎ 800/241-0824, 305/891-4117 or 649/946-2321.

❄ January

New Year's Day, public holiday.

❄ March

Commonwealth Day is a public holiday held on a Monday in early March.

Spring Garden Festival, Grand Turk. Held during Easter, this celebration includes kite-flying, a candlelight evening ceremony on Good Friday, a local restaurant competition and a fish fry.

❄ May

Regatta, South Caicos. Held in late May, this event includes a beauty pageant, sailboat races (call the Tourist Board for information) and plenty of local food.

National Heroes Day. This public holiday takes place in late May. Most offices close for this day.

❄ June

Queen's Official Birthday Celebrations, Grand Turk, This public holiday takes place in early June. Special events include a uniformed parade, featuring everyone from the police force to the Girl Scout group. There's also a presentation of medals from Her Majesty the Queen.

Fun in the Sun, Salt Cay. Late June. Fun includes a beauty pageant for some of the islands' youngest residents, dances and local food.

⁘ July

Annual Billfish Tournament, Provo. Mid-July. Call the Tourist Board for details.

Festarama, North Caicos. Mid-July. local bands play and sports events are held.

Provo Summer Festival, Provo. Late July. Miss Turks & Caicos beauty pageant, dinghy races and parades.

Grand Turk Fishing Tournament, Grand Turk. Late July. This event begins with parties, a beach volleyball tournament and music before getting down to serious business – fishing. Competitors vie for a top prize of $5,000. To enter, anglers must register and pay fees before the start of the event. For information, ☎ 649/946-2504.

⁘ August

Middle Caicos Expo, Middle Caicos. Mid-August. Includes beauty pageants, boat races and sports events.

Rake and Scrape Music Festival, Grand Turk. Mid-August. Musicians playing drums and handsaws!

Cactusfest, Grand Turk. This late-August celebration features parades, local bands and games.

Turks & Caicos

⁙ September

National Youth Day, all islands. Late September. Sports are the main theme of this annual event that celebrates the young of the island.

⁙ October

Turks and Caicos Amateur Open Golf Championship, Provo. Mid-October. This 36-hole, two-day championship is open to visitors. Contact the Tourist Board for details, or speak with the Provo Golf Club at ☎ 649/946-5991, fax 649/946-5992.

Columbus Day Celebrations, Grand Turk. Mid-October.

Columbus Day, all islands. This public holiday takes place on October 13.

International Human Rights Day, all islands. A public holiday. October 24.

⁙ November

Remembrance Day, Grand Turk. November 2.

Burning of Guy Fawkes, all islands. November 5. This popular British tradition involves the burning of a straw Guy Fawkes, the man who attempted to blow up Parliament.

⁙ December

Christmas Tree Lighting Ceremony, Grand Turk. Early December. A public lighting of the island Christams tree kicks off the start of the holiday season.

Christmas Day. Public holiday. December 25.

Boxing Day. National holiday. December 26. Traditionally, this day was when servants were given boxed leftovers from their masters' Christmas dinner and were allowed to celebrate on their own.

Watchnight, all islands. December 31. This longtime tradition includes an all-night church service featuring the ringing of bells to welcome the new year.

Turks & Caicos

Appendix

Tasting By Mail

❧ Hot Sauces

Gourmet International Distributors, Inc., ☎ 800/273-7252; www.hotsauceetc.com; E-mail info@hotsauceetc.com. Gourmet International sells Pickappeppa sauce (both brown and red), Walker's Wood jerk sauce and more.

Jamaica Standard Products Company Ltd., ☎ 800/240-6043; www.caribplace.com/foods/jspcl.htm; E-mail sanco@colis. com. Baronhall farms products, including Hell Hot Pepper Concentrate, Scotch Bonnet Pepper Sauce and Jamaican Hot Curry Sauce, are sold through this company.

❧ Spices

World Harbors, www.maine.com/worldharbors. This site offers sauces and marinades.

Travel Information

Check out these Internet sites and mail order companies. They offer a selection of items that will enable you to bring home a taste of the islands any time.

www.grand-bahama.com – The official website of the Grand Bahama Island Tourism Board. Information on where to stay, what to do, nature and even a newsgroup to hear from other Bahamas travelers.

www.bahamas.net – Traveler's information, government info, real estate, dining, shopping, hotels, calendar of events.

www.thebahamas.com – Facts, hotels, shopping, dining. Travel guide to Nassau, Paradise Island, Bimini and Abaco.

www.gobahamas.com – Official website of the Islands of The Bahamas. Information on the history of these islands, how to get there, the people of The Bahamas, where to stay, travel tips, tourist offices, doing business in The Bahamas and more.

www.bahamasweb.com – This site includes a tourist guide, restaurant guide, hotel information, weather and more.

Conversion Charts

Measurement Equivalents

Metric:

¼ teaspoon~ ~ ~ ~ ~ ~ ~ ~ ~ 1 milliliter rounded

½ teaspoon ~ ~ ~ ~ ~ ~ ~ ~ ~ 2 milliliter rounded

1 teaspoon ~ ~ ~ ~ ~ ~ ~ ~ ~ ~ ~ ~ 5 milliliters

1 tablespoon ~ ~ ~ ~ ~ ~ ~ ~ 15 milliliters rounded

¼ cup ~ ~ ~ ~ ~ ~ ~ ~ ~ ~ ~ ~ ~ ~ 65 milliliters

½ cup ~ ~ ~ ~ ~ ~ ~ ~ ~ ~ ~ ~ ~ ~ 125 milliliters

⅔ cup ~ ~ ~ ~ ~ ~ ~ ~ ~ ~ ~ ~ ~ ~ 165 milliliters

¾ cup ~ ~ ~ ~ ~ ~ ~ ~ ~ ~ ~ ~ ~ ~ 185 milliliters

1 cup ~ ~ ~ ~ ~ ~ ~ ~ ~ ~ ~ ~ ~ ~ ~ 250 milliliters

300° F ~ ~ ~ ~ ~ ~ ~ ~ ~ ~ ~ ~ ~ ~ ~ ~ ~ ~ 150° C

325° F ~ ~ ~ ~ ~ ~ ~ ~ ~ ~ ~ ~ ~ ~ ~ ~ ~ ~ 165° C

350° F ~ ~ ~ ~ ~ ~ ~ ~ ~ ~ ~ ~ ~ ~ ~ ~ ~ ~ 180° C

375° F ~ ~ ~ ~ ~ ~ ~ ~ ~ ~ ~ ~ ~ ~ ~ ~ ~ ~ 190° C

400° F ~ ~ ~ ~ ~ ~ ~ ~ ~ ~ ~ ~ ~ ~ ~ ~ ~ ~ 200° C

425° F ~ ~ ~ ~ ~ ~ ~ ~ ~ ~ ~ ~ ~ ~ ~ ~ ~ ~ 215° C

450° F ~ ~ ~ ~ ~ ~ ~ ~ ~ ~ ~ ~ ~ ~ ~ ~ ~ ~ 230° C

475° F ~ ~ ~ ~ ~ ~ ~ ~ ~ ~ ~ ~ ~ ~ ~ ~ ~ ~ 240° C

1 pound ~ ~ ~ ~ ~ ~ ~ ~ ~ ~ ~ ~ 0.454 kilograms

1 ounce ~ ~ ~ ~ ~ ~ ~ ~ ~ ~ ~ ~ ~ ~ 28.3 grams

Margarine/Butter:

¼ cup ~ ~ ~ ~ ~ ~ ~ ~ ~ ~ ~ ~ ~ ½ stick (⅛ pound)

½ cup ~ ~ ~ ~ ~ ~ ~ ~ ~ ~ ~ ~ ~ ~ 1 stick (¼ pound)

1 cup ~ ~ ~ ~ ~ ~ ~ ~ ~ ~ ~ ~ ~ ~ 2 sticks (½ pound)

2 cups ~ ~ ~ ~ ~ ~ ~ ~ ~ ~ ~ ~ ~ 4 sticks (1 pound)

Miscellaneous:

3 teaspoons ~ ~ ~ ~ ~ ~ ~ ~ ~ ~ ~ ~ 1 tablespoon

2 tablespoons ~ ~ ~ ~ ~ ~ ~ ~ ~ ~ ~ ~ ~ ~ ⅛ cup

5 tablespoons ~ ~ ~ ~ ~ ~ ~ ~ ~ ~ ~ ~ ~ ~ ⅓ cup

8 tablespoons ~ ~ ~ ~ ~ ~ ~ ~ ~ ~ ~ ~ ~ ~ ½ cup

12 tablespoons ~ ~ ~ ~ ~ ~ ~ ~ ~ ~ ~ ~ ~ ~ ¾ cup

16 tablespoons ~ ~ ~ ~ ~ ~ ~ ~ ~ ~ ~ ~ ~ ~ 1 cup

1 cup ~ ~ ~ ~ ~ ~ ~ ~ ~ ~ ~ ~ ~ ~ ~ ~ ~ ½ pint

2 cups ~ ~ ~ ~ ~ ~ ~ ~ ~ ~ ~ ~ ~ ~ ~ ~ ~ 1 pint

4 cups ~ ~ ~ ~ ~ ~ ~ ~ ~ ~ ~ ~ ~ ~ ~ ~ ~ 1 quart

2 pints ~ ~ ~ ~ ~ ~ ~ ~ ~ ~ ~ ~ ~ ~ ~ ~ ~ 1 quart

4 quarts ~ ~ ~ ~ ~ ~ ~ ~ ~ ~ ~ ~ ~ ~ ~ ~ 1 gallon

Appendix

Conversion Factors

Ounces to grams: *multiply ounce figure by 28.3.*

Grams to ounces: *multiply gram figure by .0353.*

Pounds to kilograms: *multiply pound figure by 0.454.*

Ounces to milliliters: *multiply ounce figure by 30.*

Cups to liters: *multiply cup figure by 0.24.*

Fahrenheit to Celsius: *subtract 32 from the Fahrenheit figure, multiply by 5, then divide by 9.*

Celsius to Fahrenheit: *multiply Celsius figure by 9, divide by 5, then add 32.*

Inches to centimeters: *multiply inch figure by 2.54.*

Centimeters to inches: *multiply centimeter figure by 0.39.*

Bibliography

Baker, Christopher P. *Bahamas, Turks and Caicos.* Lonely Planet, 1998.

Blount, Steve and Lisa Walker. *Diving and Snorkeling Guide to The Bahamas, Nassau and New Providence Island.* Pisces Books, 1990.

Charles, Ron. *Bahamas Guide.* Open Road, 1997.

Cohen, Steve, Janet Groene, Laurie Werner, Ute Vladimir, et al. *Caribbean: The Greater Antilles, Bermuda, Bahamas.* Nelles Verlage 1997.

Dulles, Wink and Marael Johnson. *The Bahamas.* Fielding Worldwide, 1996.

Fleming, Carol B. *Adventuring in the Caribbean: The Sierra Club Travel Guide to the 40 Islands of the Caribbean Sea in-*

cluding The Bahamas, Jamaica and the Dominican Republic. Sierra Club Books, 1989.

Frommer, Arthur and Porter, Darwin. *Frommer's Bahamas 2000.* IDG Books, 1999.

Guttermann, Steve and Philip Z. Trupp. *Diver's Almanac: Guide to The Bahamas and Caribbean.* Triton Publishing, 1987.

Harris, Richard and Lynn Seldon. *Hidden Bahamas.* Ulysses Press, 1997.

Henderson, James S. *The Caribbean and The Bahamas, 4th Edition.* Cadogan, 1997.

Howard, Blair. *Adventure Guide to The Bahamas.* Hunter Publishing, 1999.

Huber, Joyce and Jon Huber. *Best Dives of The Bahamas, Bermuda, the Florida Keys and Turks & Caicos.* Hunter Publishing, 2000.

Huber, Joyce and Jon Huber. *Best Dives' Snorkeling Adventures: A Guide to The Bahamas, Bermuda, Caribbean, Hawaii and Florida Keys.* Photographics Publishing, 1998.

Jeffrey, Nan. *Bahamas: Out Island Odyssey.* Menasha Ridge Press, 1995.

Keller, Bob and Charlotte Keller. *Diving and Snorkeling Guide to The Bahamas Family Islands and Grand Bahama.* Pisces Books, 1994.

McMorran, Jennifer. *Ulysses Travel Guide of The Bahamas.* Ulysses Books, 1998.

Pavlidis, Stephen J. *The Exuma Guide: A Cruising Guide to the Exuma Cays: Approaches, Routes, Anchorages, Dive Sights, Flora, Fauna and Lore of the Exuma Cays.* Seaworthy Publications, 1997.

Pavlidis, Stephen J. *On and Off the Beaten Path: The Central Southern Bahamas from South Florida to the Turks and Caicos.* Seaworthy Publications, 1998.

Permenter, P & Bigley, J. *Nassau & The Best of The Bahamas Alive!* Hunter Publishing, 2000.

Porter, Darwin. *The Bahamas.* Frommer, 1997.

Wilson, Matthew. *The Bahamas Cruising Guide.* McGraw-Hill, 1998.

Recipe Index

Index